Tony Jacklin

THE FIRST FORTY YEARS

Tony Jacklin

THE FIRST FORTY YEARS

Tony Jacklin with Renton Laidlaw

Macdonald
Queen Anne Press

A *Queen Anne Press* BOOK

© Birdies Limited

First published in 1985 by
Queen Anne Press, a division of
Macdonald & Co (Publishers) Ltd,
Maxwell House, 74 Worship Street,
London EC2A 2EN

A BPCC plc Company

British Library Cataloguing in Publication Data

Jacklin, Tony
  Tony Jacklin The First Forty Years
  1. Golfers—Great Britain—Biography
  2. Jacklin, Tony
  I. Title   II. Laidlaw, Renton
  796.352'092'4   GV964.J3

ISBN 0–356–10638–1

Typeset by C. Leggett & Son Ltd
Mitcham, Surrey
Printed and bound in Great Britain by
Hazell, Watson & Viney Limited
Member of the BPCC Group
Aylesbury, Bucks

Contents

1
The Early Days

There have been times when I have been so disenchanted with my form that I have not really wanted to go to the golf course at all, but looking back on a 20 year career from the venerable age of 41 I'll admit readily that golf has been good to me . . . particularly good to me. It has afforded me a lifestyle I could never have envisaged as a youngster in Scunthorpe, coming as I did from a relatively poor family whose only concession to luxury was the fact that we owned a car when most of our neighbours did not. It so happens that the impression that left on me caused me in later life to become something of a car collector—owning a large car represented to me a physical manifestation of success.

Over the past 20 years I have met and played—and sometimes beaten—the best golfers in the world. I have played with some of the greatest personalities in business and politics and from the entertainment world, and I have loved it. I do not enjoy being the centre of attention (although I have had to learn to cope with this aspect of stardom) but I do enjoy mixing and talking to men and women whose influence is great. I'm no snob—at least I hope I'm not—but there is nothing I enjoy more than a stimulating discussion over dinner (and after it) with the conversation helped along with a good bottle of Margaux and a vintage port. That to me is all part of the stylish life I have been able to afford because of two great weeks in my career: a July week at Lytham St Annes in 1969, when I became the first British player for eighteen years to win the Open; and less than a year later a week at Hazeltine in America when I won the second largest event in world golf—the US Open. I had the world at my feet then and if, on looking back, I cannot help but be annoyed at the way I allowed my schedule to be manipulated, I can reflect that it was after all probably my own fault. I could have said 'no' more often when the offers to play around the world flooded in, but when you come from a background where money was always tight maybe I can forgive myself for chasing the pounds and dollars so relentlessly, so myopically, that all the fun went out of the game for me for a time.

If only I had stopped long enough to think about what was happening to me it might have been different, but the price of success is always a costly one in terms of human relations unless you happen to be very lucky indeed. One only has to look at what success has done to so many of our top entertainers in terms of ruined marriages, and drink and drug problems; or at what success brought for that brilliant sportsman George Best, who could not cope with the triumphs and, sadly, did not have the personal discipline to enjoy the rewards his talented feet and soccer brain brought him. I'm lucky I've never had problems of this kind. Maybe I am tougher mentally than most, maybe there is something in my make-up which has prevented me from pressing the self-destruct button. Maybe—but there is also Vivien. We have been married 19 years and she has provided the stability of a happy family life to help keep my feet on the ground.

When we got married I remember telling her that I hoped she knew what she was letting herself in for. She was marrying a golfer, an ambitious one at that. I wanted to be the best in the world and that would mean that golf would take top priority in my life even ahead of her. She accepted those conditions and now 20 years on it is Vivien and the family that have priority over anything else I do. It has come full circle. She has shared the marvellous moments of international success with me and suffered the agonies with me when I went through a massive form slump and became so mentally obsessed with my inability to hole putts that I would lie awake at night searching for the solution. Not that we have ever talked a great deal about golf when I have got home. I am one of the lucky ones who can switch off when I have walked off the eighteenth green and completed the press interviews. Not always, of course, but most of the time, and that has been as important to me as the ability to switch my concentration on and off as and when required. It's easy to concentrate, of course, when you are playing well . . . more difficult when you are not. Then the slightest movement in the crowd, the tiniest click of a camera, can and has put me off.

Perhaps in the past seven or eight years I have earned a reputation for myself as a moaner, complaining regularly about almost everything, but then I have always been a perfectionist. Unless everything is just right I am unhappy, and for me playing golf in the last few years has been nothing but frustration, frustration eased from time to time with a victory which kept me going when I might otherwise have decided to call it quits. Not that that would have been popular with the British fans, many of whom still feel let down by the fact that I did not go on and win more and more majors. Ten years ago I worried about the responsibility I felt I had to give the fans what they wanted—birdies and eagles and runaway victories. Today I'm far more circumspect. What the hell! I've done what no other British golfer has done in 65 years—held (if only for a month in 1970) the British and American Open Championships. I've done that. No one can take that away from me. Now, at 41, I don't give a damn what people think. Now Tony Jacklin pleases himself and, frankly, I feel I deserve to. I certainly have no conscience about it. I do not owe anybody anything these days, except my family and myself, which does not mean, of course, that I do not operate in the only way I know, giving of my best in business, playing hard in those events in which I choose to compete (fewer and fewer, even if I have no intention of quitting the tournament scene yet), and taking time to learn about the skills of golf commentating in my new enjoyable role with BBC Television.

I'm a natural worrier. I would worry if I felt I was not giving value for money—and remember as a former Open champion I still receive substantial appearance money when I play around the world. Integrity is important in life. I am very conscious of it, which is not to say that looking back I cannot remember occasions when I've let someone down. I can—but hopefully it was not too often. You cannot go through life pleasing everyone, and there is in my make-up a toughness, a single-mindedness, a strong belief in my own ability to make the right decision, a cockiness, a selfish determination which helped me win two majors but which has sometimes created the wrong impression . . . and lost me friends.

Whatever anyone else thinks, I happen to believe that I am quite a nice fellow! (But I suppose I am bound to be biased.) I like having people around in small numbers—six or eight to dinner. Any more than that and I prefer them behind the ropes. I have not changed in a clubhouse for fifteen years, and have not been in a public bar for as long—I just cannot afford to because I feel that someone, with the confidence that one or two pints can give, may come up to start an argument about something. I don't miss it. My life is now centred on the home—a new one, as it turns out, down at Sotogrande in southern Spain, a house which I helped design myself. It is my base for the start of the second 20 years of my career, two decades I am looking forward to with all the enthusiasm I had when I first embarked on the international golf scene in the mid '60s.

I have an interest in a development company in which my brother-in-law is one of my partners—he built his own home at Scunthorpe—I have a golf-cart business that is going well and there is the excitement of having my own club and course. My aim is to have £2 million in the bank by the time I am 50. I used to say I had enough to see me and the family through my lifetime but now I'm not so sure, what with inflation and current conditions. If everything goes well I think I will achieve that target. Certainly I shall be giving it the same enthusiastic shot I gave my golf.

It is hard to imagine what has happened to me since those days when, as a well-built youngster, I started playing the game . . . and amazingly only by sheer chance. Eric Markee, who lived next door to us in Collinson Avenue, decided to have a go at golf and asked my father Arthur to have a go with him. I don't know where they got the clubs—hired them I suppose—but my dad got hooked and so, it turned out, did I. I was eight or nine at the time and honestly no one in our family had ever given golf a moment's thought. There were two courses in Scunthorpe but none of us knew where they were—if we had ever passed them, we had not noticed them. It was not the kind of game families in our street got interested in—in those days at any rate. I suspect everyone in the street plays now.

I never had a full set of clubs until I was eighteen, and I got them from the Dunlop company after I had become assistant to Bill Shankland at Potters Bar. When I started off I used my father's set to hit shots, but only when I was out of sight of the clubhouse because the club members were not too keen on youngsters playing—well, few clubs are. It makes me laugh a bit when I think of some of the members who showed no interest in helping me when I was a lad but after I had won the Open came up to shake my hand and tell me they always knew I would be a good 'un—but that's life.

I remember how excited I was when I got my own first few clubs—cut-down hickories they were, so you know how old they would have been. Being hickory they could be shortened by using nothing more technical than a saw and my dad, sensing that my interest in the game was more than casual, did the necessary. Maybe Ted Muscroft, the pro, helped him because around this time I spent every possible minute at the Scunthorpe club with Ted. I helped in the shop, I drove the tractor, cut the greens and played golf—or rather hit shots—in the afternoons. With hindsight, I was also lucky in having someone of about my own age to play with at that time. Frank Barclay was a year older but just as enthusiastic and we did a great deal together. It is always easier to do something if you have a pal—going to the dancing, the pictures, the snooker hall or, in our case, the golf course. I usually won and I know how much I enjoyed winning even then, although the competitive instinct was not fully honed at that time. I was just intrigued by the game, desperately anxious to develop a swing that would work.

I read all the magazines but curiously my father never bought me a golf instruction book. I don't have one in my library, indeed I do not have an extensive library. Some people swear by Ben Hogan's famous book *Five Lessons:*

The Modern Fundamentals of Golf and even go to the lengths of carrying it around in their golf bags for instant perusal when something goes wrong. They must be crazy to think that they can sort out their problem that easily. I perfected my swing and my grip by trial and error in the early days, until I was happy with what I had and felt that it would enable me to become a winner. You can call it instinct if you like but I just happen to have been lucky enough to have got it almost right as an amateur. My swing has not changed all that much in the past 20 years (but my grip has because it needed to be changed). Every good player who came to play at the club became my instant target. I offered to caddy for them in order to learn more about how they handled themselves on the course—I studied what we would now call their course management.

I was so keen on the game that my mother never worried about where I was. She knew. I was up early in the morning—I'm a morning person—made up a sandwich and cycled off to the club, staying there sometimes twelve hours and in winter until it was dark. To sharpen up my short game I would take with me an umbrella and a bundle of firewood. I would stick the umbrella in the ground and place the firewood around it to make a big circle. Then I would take a bag of 50 balls and try to hit 20 or 30 into the circle and would not stop until I had. I enjoyed it just as Severiano Ballesteros used to enjoy playing golf with his borrowed 3-iron at about the same age down in Pedrena near Santander. I would imagine I was being watched all the time by Ben Hogan or by Sam Snead. I was trying to impress them in my golfing imagination but when I achieved my target there was no one there to pat me on the shoulders or shake my hand. Yet I was not too disappointed. I may be a dreamer and have a fertile imagination but there is a massive streak of realism in my character as well. I knew the applause could come later.

Sometimes I played with Ted and my father and for long enough I found it tough to break 90, but then one day playing on my own I shot 84. I was so delighted I rushed in to tell Ted, who right-hooked me metaphorically by saying he did not believe me. That afternoon I played again, with Ted this

time, and again shot 84. It was raining heavily. It was a
miserably grey day but I'd shown him I was no liar. When I
was thirteen I broke 80 for the first time and then hardly
ever scored above 80 after that. I was ready for a handicap
and put in three cards, significantly—on my father's
advice—putting in three of my poorer cards, including a 90
and a 91, to get a better rating. There were no junior
handicaps, of course, just senior ratings because the club
members didn't want juniors around their feet.

I was too young then to resent the attitude of the
members, who for the most part were a gigantic pain in the
neck, but I get angry today when I see how some clubs treat
their junior members—the youngsters who will become the
lifeblood of the club in the years to follow. I suppose it is the
old British habit of adopting an attitude based on the
principle that young people should not have it any easier
than their elders had it 30 or 40 years earlier. It really is a
head-in-the-sand attitude and is still all too prevalent. The
world is full of remarkably selfish people—life's takers. I
know a great many nice people but my general opinion of
human beings is not great. Too many people think only of
themselves all the time. They go through life grabbing but
never giving.

Wanted or not, at Scunthorpe I got my handicap and
quickly started working on reducing it. I had to hit the ball
straight because although the course was flat and parkland
in character there were a great many trees. It was very
narrow. Looking back, it is a wonder I did not get fed up
with the game because of the rows I used to have with my
dad, who always felt he knew better than me. As a kid I
suppose I should have expected him to know best, but when
it came to golf I was clear in my own mind about what was
right and wrong for me, if only because I had practised so
much to perfect my method. My dad kept giving me obvious
bits of advice which infuriated me—daft advice like saying
'nice and smooth' as I was just about to hit the ball. I'd gone
through that routine in my mind before. You know I think he
only realised my potential as a golfer when I began to beat
him. We never played for money because we didn't have
any. He did not even give my sister Lynn or me pocket

money. I had to work for my money, doing a paper round in the mornings and, at the weekends, working at Scunthorpe market helping Irving Ballante auction off cheap towels, sheets, clocks and that kind of thing. I made £2 a week but never used it to buy balls or golf equipment. The balls I used I found by hunting through the rough at the course— fortunately a good few members sprayed a lot of drives!

Money was tight in those days. What I earned I used to finance my visits to Binns snooker hall, which has long since been pulled down. I was good at snooker and of course I played a nifty game of soccer but golf was my passion and I was beginning to play more and more with some of the members. On one occasion I was down so much on bets that I remember taking a micrometer—for measuring the thickness of steel—up to the club to try and flog it to pay off my debts. I don't think I managed to sell it but I must have got the money from somewhere because I kept on playing. I'd been given the micrometer by my uncle because the general feeling was that I would become an apprentice fitter at the steelworks . . . even if I had other ideas. I never told my uncle I had sold it, of course.

I, meanwhile, was dreaming of becoming a professional golfer. As a youngster and still today I can get terrific inspiration from thinking about what might be. It was a dream of mine that one day I might go to America to play golf there and be a marvellous success. I had been fortunate enough to be taken to Lindrick in 1957, when Dai Rees led his British team to success in the Ryder Cup. The only pro I had known until then was dear old Ted Muscroft (now incidentally down at Newquay—we still keep in touch). With the best will in the world he was never better than 8 handicap as a golfer, so I longed for the British Tour, which was nothing like as extensive as it is today, to come near our area. The Ryder Cup was the chance for me to see the real players in action—in 1957 there were Peter Alliss and Max Faulkner, Bernard Hunt, Eric Brown, Ken Bousfield, Christy O'Connor, the late Harry Weetman and Dai Rees, and the American side included Dow Finsterwald, Tommy Bolt and Dick Mayer. They had only been names in magazines, headline-stealers in the newspapers for me until

Lindrick when I had the chance to see them actually perform, and walk with them, even if I did not get to speak to them—I have never asked for an autograph in my life although I have spent hours signing mine, and am happy to do so. The name Tony Jacklin looks and sounds great now but at one time I hated it. My mother had planned anyway to call me Anthony but a nurse who picked me up just after I was born gave me the nickname Ten-ton Tony because I was a heavy baby, and it stuck!

Later on, as a teenager, I remember complaining at dinner one night that Tony Jacklin did not have the ring of a Ben Hogan or a Sam Snead or an Arnold Palmer. These I insisted were great names. Yours will be too I was told—and happily my parents were right. When I returned from Lindrick—inspired—it was light enough for me to be dropped off at the club, and I remember producing one of my best ever nine-holes scores. Golf had a vice-like grip on me. Even if I had wanted to give it up (which I did not) it would not have let me. I was hooked and ready for a bigger challenge.

It had cost my father £6 a year and me £2 as a junior at Scunthorpe but I needed stronger opposition and the only place to get that was at Holme Hall, where there were a few better players, some of whom included me in their regular games. We used to play for what I considered a fortune then—half a crown (12½p these days). There was Frank Cottingham who used to make washers and driers, Bill Empson the car dealer, and Alan Williamson. If I lost I paid up, but very quickly I was winning more than I lost even if my grip was a bit strong in those days, causing me occasionally to hook wildly. Playing with the older fellows helped me mature as a golfer and as a person. More and more I was sure that my future lay outdoors on the international tournament scene and not indoors at a lathe in the Scunthorpe Steel Mills. Convincing parents is less easy. I tried but was signed on as an apprentice fitter when I was fifteen.

If my parents believed I had talent as a golfer they were not prepared to encourage me too much to make it my career—for one thing it would mean my leaving home.

15

They wanted to ensure I had steady employment, a good basic trade, before gambling on golf, and I do not doubt their motives; but the time I spent in the Scunthorpe steelworks, where my father worked as a lorry driver, was among my most unhappy. I could not wait to dash from the factory to the clubhouse. I was earning £3 11s 3d at the steelworks but eventually my parents realised that it was never going to work there, and I got a job with a local solicitor, Eric Kemp, who was a member at Holme Hall. I delivered a few letters in the morning, hung around reception until early afternoon and then headed for the golf course. And he paid me almost double what I had been receiving a week as an apprentice fitter. It made sense all round.

My game was improving all the time. At thirteen I had won the Lincolnshire Junior Championship, which was open to golfers up to the age of eighteen—indeed I was the youngest junior champion and went on to win it three more times. Two years later I won the Lincolnshire County Championship on a wild windy day over Holme Hall. I did enjoy winning that one because all the local professionals played as well. The junior events in those early days were small affairs. I remember one time the total County entry was just eight juniors. Today there would be a minimum of eight from almost every club in the area—an indication of the growth of the game in the past 25 years. I was good enough by the time I was fifteen to be playing in the county side against Yorkshire, Northamptonshire and Norfolk. I did enjoy playing at Brancaster and Hunstanton but travelling around was a costly business. Again I was lucky and I needed to be. In the early '60s team members did not get expenses. Maybe it was a sign of things to come but Bill Bloomer, father of the tennis star Shirley Bloomer, used to take me to matches in his Bentley. The original idea I think was that I could drive it home and let him have a more relaxed time but, of course, I was too young to have a licence. I loved the smell of the leather upholstery in the car and dreamed more than ever of one day owning such a car myself.

Secretly I wrote off to California applying for the job of an assistant but not surprisingly I got no reply. My father and mother never knew. I'm an ambitious fellow and I was not getting on quickly enough. To be frank I was becoming more and more frustrated. I was wasting time, going nowhere fast. If I had had more and even tougher competition when I was younger I guess I could have done what Severiano Ballesteros was doing at nineteen—win tournaments on the professional scene. It is easier now for talented youngsters to come through—the route is fairly clearly defined. In 1962 it was not. I was bubbling over with confidence, cocky without being cheeky, and eighteen years old. Every week I would scan the advertisements in *Golf Illustrated*. One day I spotted that Bill Shankland at Potters Bar was looking for an assistant. I knew I needed to go outside Lincolnshire because only one club in the whole county had an assistant—and that was Woodhall Spa. I wrote off and received a reply. I persuaded my father that it would be worth while driving me down for the interview.

At first he was annoyed that I had written away behind his back but, by now, my folks knew that golf was to be my career. I was more certain than ever but I promised my father that if he felt the Potters Bar job was not right for me I would not take it if offered. Shankland offered me £6 a week, plus half of what I made teaching and playing and I jumped at it. My father agreed and I prepared to leave home . . . and what drama that caused. You would have thought I was leaving never to return or heading for the other end of the world instead of just 100 miles south.

My new billet was with Mrs Baker, who lived in an end terraced house not far from the course. She charged £3 15s a week, and made fantastic breakfasts. I signed up for two weeks . . . and stayed for seven years. Vivien and I even went there after we were married. She was a fantastic person and I was always sorry that when Eamonn Andrews did 'This Is Your Life' with me (grabbing me when I came out of Buckingham Palace after receiving my OBE from the Queen) Mrs Baker was not on. She should have been but then I had known nothing about the programme, which came as a total surprise to me. On reflection the years I spent with Mrs Baker were the happiest years of my life. She had a son who was ten years older and we used to go round to the local to play darts. I was in the local team. Mrs Baker's husband Fred drove over a million miles for London Transport. He's dead now but Mrs Baker is still alive. They were great, great people. There was always a good atmosphere in the house and they were interested in what I was doing. She fussed around me a bit and I enjoyed that—I loved being with the Bakers as much as I often hated being part of Bill Shankland's staff. He was a big blustery ex Rugby League international from Australia who called a spade a bloody shovel, and not surprisingly our personalities clashed. Only he was older and usually won. Still he gave me the grounding I needed for the big time . . . and that was not far off. I had marked time long enough. I was ready to go.

2
Joining the Professionals

I went to join Bill Shankland in January 1962. I was eighteen years old and impatient for success. I used to hate him. He criticised me continually and worked me like a cart horse. He had three or four assistants during 1963, for instance, but I was the only one there all the time and it was me who did the books, me who did the ordering, me who swept out the shop, and all for £6 a week plus a small amount I earned by teaching and playing. We had big arguments but he spent time with me too, helped me with my game, hardened my attitude.

I grew up under Bill Shankland but found his teaching a little confusing. He would tell me to do one thing one day, another the next. There are, of course, a thousand ways of saying the same thing in golf—involving the hips, the knees, the legs, the shoulders, the upper body, the head, the feet—but frankly after a week or so I felt he had chopped and changed my game so much that I had to learn to sift the information he gave me carefully. One day he would tell me the importance of hitting from the right, the next day he would be advocating I pull down from the left . . . so I worked simply on picking his brain. He had hundreds of stories to tell and told them well. Often we would sit in his back shop while he recalled incidents and experiences with Charlie Compston and Eddie Whitcombe. The past came alive for him then, and for us too. The stories only made me more eager to make it big and show Bill Shankland that I meant business—and I did, eventually taking much pleasure in driving my first Rolls-Royce into the parking spot beside his shop at the club. Curiously, the burning desire to prove my point to Bill had been my inspiration, yet when I achieved success it gave me little or no satisfaction to show him I had made it! What Bill Shankland did, however, was toughen me up for the tournament front line and I was nearly ready to go, even if I had no money.

Three months after going to Potters Bar I won the Middlesex Assistants' Championships at Northwood, and Dunlop rang up to offer me a brand new set of clubs—or rather they offered them to me through Bill Shankland. I was thrilled and did not mind handing in my own ill-matched set to Bill who had indicated Dunlop would like to give them to an up-and-coming youngster. I thought that was a great idea and expressed the view that I was sorry no one had done it for me.

I never gave any member cause to complain about me, and did my duties around the shop, but what I wanted to do was play. So in 1964, a year after Bill stopped me going to South Africa for some winter-sunshine golf because he claimed I was not 'ready', I decided to quit. I did not mince my words. I have always believed in plain talking. I said I would not work for him even for £100 a week. He went quiet and so too did I. It was so different from the incident two years earlier when, just weeks into the new job, I had written asking Keith Hockey if I could join him at Muswell Hill. Shankland had found out about this because Hockey telephoned to make some enquiries. There was a right shouting match after that. This time it was different. He sensed I meant to leave and I did . . . but he took the trouble to telephone the club president, Johnny Rubens, who was big in property. He never played on a Friday morning but he did the week I resigned just to put a new proposal to me. If I would stay attached to the club they would pay my wages, or at least they would pay to Bill what Bill paid to me. In addition the club agreed to sponsor me at the few tournaments I played. (The circuit then was very different from the £4 million PGA European Tour now offering huge prizes at events from April through to November.) I did, however, want to go to South Africa where they played during our winter. I had saved £340 and decided to put £200 of this towards the trip. The club, or rather Johnny Rubens, and Eric Hayes of Dunlop put up the balance and I was off, full of hope. I spent the money—some £600—and I made £35! Shankland's view that I was not ready had been justified, yet I had in 1963 at Lytham managed to finish thirty-first in the Open. That was the year I borrowed £5 from a Potters Bar member to avoid hitchhiking home.

One thing I had learned very early is that you have to pay for your experience. The year I paid out £600 to go to South Africa and won £35 you could say I lost £565 on paper but I looked at it very differently. I reckoned I had paid out £565 for the experience of playing on different grasses, on different courses, in a different climate and conditions. I was young and taking everything on board to use it, hopefully, in the long term to make the grade on the main British circuit. I would not, looking back, do anything differently. I was confident in one respect but not as far as tournament play was concerned. I wanted to have an old head on young shoulders but to get that old head I needed to suffer a little bit. I needed experience and it was great getting it in South Africa, although I had a narrow escape in a car smash when the car in which Tommy Horton, Lionel Platts and I were travelling somersaulted off the road. Lionel Platts was the most badly shaken but I crawled out, got a lift to the course and shot a 69. I did not make a lot of halfway cuts but we met a whole lot of nice people at Kimberley and Johannesburg. We were taking chances because we all wanted to get on. We all knew the world would not come to us. We knew if we sat at home with our feet up nothing would happen.

Opportunity does not knock on your door. You have to go out and find it. It is a philosophy of mine that you get the rewards in life in direct proportion to the work you put into it. What amazes me is that so many people who are not prepared to make sacrifices or work hard positively resent the success that comes to those that do. Maybe it is a peculiarly British trait—I don't know, but I often feel that the harder anyone tries in this country the more likely he is to be sniped at by those who would not travel to the other end of their town for a job.

Down in South Africa Gary Player helped me a bit too—but only on the periphery. He was a demi-god and I was a nobody in golfing terms, looking for a reputation but learning too about homesickness. I remember being invited by friends to stay on a week after the Safari Tour to go to the Kruger National Park. I was homesick and declined. Twenty-four hours later I was back in Britain in sub-zero temperatures and realising what a fool I had been. I cannot stand the cold weather which is one reason why I enjoy living in Spain where the climate is altogether more comfortable. Today I have cut my travel down to the minimum. I'm basically a home-bird, anyway, enjoying my new life with the family I saw growing up. So many of my colleagues missed seeing their children grow up. In a way I was lucky. My success enabled me to make a conscious effort to stay with them more and when I ran into all my putting troubles it was a further incentive, curiously enough, to stay home.

In my first full year on the British Tour I made £1,408 and the same season flew back from America to win the Gor Ray Assistants Championship. I nearly pulled out of that but Mark Wilson, the experienced golf writer of the *Evening Standard* (he is now with the *Daily Express*) persuaded me not to. I had been held up in the States at the Carling but knew I could be back for the first round of the Gor Ray if I got a later starting time. A later time would enable me to get a later plane from America. The PGA readily agreed and I headed home. I was 10 behind after 36 holes mainly as a result of jet lag—I don't really enjoy flying, for all that I have done so much—but I won! In 1966 I tied first place at Kimberley in South Africa, made £2,715 in Britain and, most important of all, ignored Henry Cotton's advice not to drink, smoke or marry until I was 25. I beat that suggested deadline by three years! I met a girl in a million.

I had come a long way along the road to success, but still had a long way to go when I travelled to Belfast for the Blaxnit Tournament and booked into the Queens Court Hotel. You have to be lucky in life sometimes. It was my luck to meet Vivien, who has all the attributes required of a pro golfer's wife, not least a reservoir of patience, never-ending tolerance and a sense of humour. I liked her the moment I saw her. I was convinced she would be my wife after our first meeting. Not everyone is that fortunate.

She has been my greatest inspiration. I had been going steady with a girl who lived not far from Mrs Baker and who had talked about marriage. I had not been sure. When I met Vivien, who was dating a member of a show band playing at the hotel, I was sure about whom I would marry! A mutual friend introduced us but Vivien declined my invitation to have a drink—not surprisingly because her boyfriend was watching her every move. I was scheduled to leave the next night but I stayed over, and although we could not have dinner we went out in the afternoon.

From then on I was miserable when we were apart. I wanted to be with her all the time so it was no surprise when we got married within seven months. It was cheaper anyway than making regular flying visits to Belfast to see her or sitting on the end of a long-distance phone call to speak to her. After we were married I did better than ever on the course! I finished third in the first three tournaments—that despite the fact that my record before was not all that good. I knew that I had done the right thing. I was nearly ready to have a go at America, but not quite—now Vivien would play her part in helping me make my final push to the top.

Vivien has been a tremendous influence on my life and it is amazing how seldom we have arguments. We seem to think along the same lines most of the time and she does give me marvellous support. She believes in me as much as I do in myself and has always been willing to do whatever I have wanted to do at any time. She happily moved from our lovely home in Lincolnshire to a manor house in Gloucestershire. Then she moved as readily from there to Jersey and then on to Sotogrande in Spain. Some wives would have been less co-operative. Indeed some wives of tour players could be said to have adversely affected their husbands' careers by their lack of a sense of adventure, but not Vivien. I'm a self-sufficient kind of person who would do well enough on a desert island, and could cope if Vivien was not there, but I'm certainly glad she is. She and the family are all the reason I need for living. I'm not religious and do not believe in an after-life. All I want to do is be remembered as a good guy, one who played well, competed honourably and looked after his family. I'd like to be remembered for that more than as the winner of the Open in 1969 or the US Open in 1970. For Vivien and I it is a partnership. She copes with all the day-to-day matters regarding the house and family. I make the major policy decisions and earn the cash. It works well.

When she married me Vivien did not know a great deal about golf but she soon learned as we headed round the world to places like New Zealand where we hitchhiked to tournaments if we were not able to organise a lift! We were that poor after paying for our flights out there. We ate only as well as the prize money I made allowed us to but we had great fun. That same year, 1966, I went to Tokyo for the World Cup—the Canada Cup as it was then. My partner in the England team was Peter Alliss and we found ourselves drawn with Arnold Palmer and Jack Nicklaus, who had won the Open that year at Muirfield. In that four-ball I was there to make up the numbers but it was me who managed to get round in 69 on the first day to take the honours. It was me who felt passionately that England could win the Cup. We did not, of course, but I was on such a high that it came as something of a shock that we were not top dogs at the end. I was that confident! I continued to improve. In 1967 I won two events in New Zealand, the Pringle Tournament at Lytham, which was to turn out to be a lucky course for me, and the Dunlop Masters at Sandwich, where my hole in one at the short sixteenth was the first ever seen on television.

People often ask whether Lytham is my very favourite course as a result of what happened there in 1969 but I have to admit it is not. I have no real favourites. I just turn up each week and play. There is nothing I can do about the venue and if I don't like a place I don't believe in fretting about something I cannot change. I am a professional and I should be able to play equally well on any course if I can play all the shots, which I can. I will admit, though, that I enjoy the surroundings of some courses more than others. I always feel much more at home, for instance, at Blackpool—surprisingly, for I know it is a horrible place. I never went to the funfairs or rode the trams or went up the

Tower but I have always felt comfortable there, especially in 1969. Maybe I enjoyed the ordinariness of the place, so different from some of the places we stayed at in America in the years before I won the Open—the formative years. These were the years before I tired of the hamburgers with chips on the side, the veal parmigianne, or the roast chicken. The plastic nature of American food contrasts so much with the rich range of haute cuisine we golfers enjoy in Europe. Later, as I struggled with my game, I found myself being pulled two ways—by logic to America where the big money was, and by preference to Europe where the money was good and I could spend more time at home. I came to hate the American way of life, the bullshit tradition, but in the late '60s, before I won the Open, it was all I expected it would be. Getting there was the realisation of what I had dreamt so many times as a youngster in Scunthorpe.

Initially, before I was there full time, I loved America. Of course Vivien and I had no family then, no responsibilities except to ourselves. We enjoyed a lively social whirl but all the time I was learning how to cope with the American courses and more especially finding out how tough it was to do well on the American scene. I used to get terribly nervous before tournaments. I lay awake in bed thinking about what might happen and could not eat any solid foods at breakfast — just raw eggs and milk. I can't remember ever being physically sick but it was awful. I used to swallow the eggs holding my nose and shutting my eyes. I knew they would give me energy and I was only too well aware of the damage that can be done to a round in the last few holes if you tire. My discomfort took some curing but I did it simply with will-power and a strong mental approach. I convinced myself that if I planned on following a career as a tournament player I could not afford to be sick the way I was. I cured it but not without difficulty. It was all part of growing up as a golfer.

I had always tried to take my golf career in logical steps. I had played at Scunthorpe Golf Club until I was the best player there, then I moved to Holme Hall and became the No. 1 golfer in the club. I won the Lincolnshire Open to be best player in the county, and when I moved to become assistant to Bill Shankland I won the Middlesex Assistants' title and then the British Assistants' crown within a couple of years. I was improving all the time, and had the important Pringle and Dunlop Masters victories behind me. I felt that it was time to try America full time. I felt I was ready. I had enjoyed my brief visits before but had decided it was useless to go there full time without having won in Europe, or Britain as it was then. I had been learning up until then, working hard on my game, practising a lot—far more than I would later on.

When I turned pro, for all that I was king pin in Lincolnshire, it turned out I was not all that good a player. I still did not really know what made it all happen. My golf was totally instinctive. I had hit so many balls during my life that it was instinct that got the job done. It was as if I was playing the piano with a hell of a lot of style but by ear and frequently improvising because I did not know enough about it to read proper music. The only way to learn was by practising hour after hour—and I did. I knew where I wanted to get to—winning the Open was the dream I had treasured for years—but I fancied I would need experience on the tough US circuit to help me achieve that. If I was still uncertain about my game I did not however lack confidence, as anyone who knew me then will tell you. I was Jack the lad. I was the fellow who always knew all the latest gags, the most risqué stories. I clearly enjoyed life and enjoyed my golf.

After I had got my Tour player's card for the American circuit in 1967 we started full belt over there the following year. By now I knew a little bit more about my swing—enough to make changes for the better. I had always been bothered about quickening my swing under pressure. I knew that human nature is such that in stress that is what happens naturally but for a long time I could not control it. It was at this time I met Tom Weiskopf and Bert Yancey and boy did these two help me get on the right track.

They made it easier for us to settle in America but more importantly helped me change my game to become more consistent. Both had tremendous talent. Tom was to go on to win the Open in 1973, but Bert's was altogether a sadder story. Having dropped out of West Point Military Academy after having a mental breakdown, he saw his golf career shattered as well. He is all right now and doing well but golf can floor a sane man, never mind someone with psychological problems. Bert really had no chance, but what a great player he was and what a good friend in the early days. I don't know how we teamed up—maybe it was kindred spirits, maybe it was the wives who brought us together. It just sort of happened the way things do on tour. We had a good time together before Bert went off the rails a couple of times due, it turned out, to a vitamin deficiency. He wanted so badly to win the US Masters and even built scale models of each hole in order to help him play the course better by getting to know it better. He came close a couple of times. Tom was very temperamental but a majestic swinger of the golf club, although he has now retired to concentrate on commentating for America's CBS company. His knowledge of the swing and Yancey's intellectual assessment of situations helped me considerably when I first joined the US Tour.

Often as we sat enjoying a Polynesian or Chinese meal—we seemed to eat a lot of them—we would talk golf for hours. We were together two or three times a week and one of the group was always doing well enough to be on a high. Golf was fun. We were enjoying it and I was gaining all the experience I needed to prepare myself for a crack at the Open—the big one. It was during those evening discussions that Weiskopf and Yancey helped me with the problem of swinging too quickly. I knew I was, but somehow could not control it. I was swinging quickly even when I felt I was not. It was costing me strokes, costing me possible victories, and I needed to have some help. I had never had a guru like Jack Grout, to whom Jack Nicklaus always returns to have his game sharpened up, or like Byron Nelson who is Tom Watson's right-hand man. Before the start of every season Watson heads for Texas for a lengthy spell with Nelson, who offered his help after Tom did well in the US Open at Winged Foot in 1974. Tom accepted and they became firm friends.

27

Being virtually self-taught I had no one to turn to until Weiskopf and Yancey offered their advice. I was not using my legs enough. My lower body action was being led by the upper body. It was necessary, said Tom, for me to slow down the upper body movements to let the legs play a more important part in the swing. It was the legs, he told me, that should lead into the shot, so I went off and practised this with a 7-iron. I hit thousands of balls! I believed what I had been told implicitly and stuck with the new method even if it was hard sometimes. I was in contention several times but failed to follow through because I was persevering with the new method and had not quite got it right. I knew it would work in the long run and my patience, my belief, paid off at Lytham. I have never reverted back to what I then considered a more comfortable method but the wrong one. The basic change I made was that I squatted a little more at address. This made me more conscious of my legs, indeed more conscious of 'hitting' the ball with different parts of the body. I started practising hitting balls with my knees. That may sound silly but I used to actually try and hit the ball with my knees and slide and turn through the shot. It worked. I became more consistent when I swung the club. Weiskopf of course had been taught by Tommy Bolt, the great Ryder Cup player who was still on tour at this time. We played regular practice rounds with him and I admired his style even if his temper and behaviour sometimes got him into trouble.

I remember Bolt had a terrible habit of breaking wind on the tee as he stood over the ball ready to hit. The officials and spectators were always shocked and finally they had to ask him not to do it. He was indignant, arguing that all the officials were doing was taking the colour out of the game. One day he told his caddy that he did not want him to talk to him as they played a round. They played silently for six holes then at the seventh, just before Bolt hit his second, the caddy tried to speak but was waved away, and Bolt went wild, shouting that he had given his orders and they had to be obeyed. Then he settled down and hit a majestic shot to 6ft. As he put the club back in the bag he said to the caddie, 'Great shot don't you think?' but the caddy did not agree, shaking his head and looking rather glum. No wonder! Bolt had hit the wrong ball!

He may have had trouble with his temper but he knew all about how to play the game in a technical sense. He was a great theorist on the use of the legs in the golf swing, and he further convinced me that I had not been using mine enough or correctly. I pumped him for information and realised the logic of his thinking.

In a stress situation, I remember he explained, the upper body is capable of moving much faster than the lower body, because the arms are smaller and lighter than the legs. So in a stress situation, with the upper body moving faster than the lower half, it is necessary to keep the upper body behind the lower body for a late hit with full power. I had to ensure that from the top of the back swing the legs were in control with the arms and hands following on. I understood that the rhythm and tempo of the swing was controlled by the legs and not by the arms and hands—something no one had even suggested to me in England. No professional I ever spoke to in Britain in the mid '60s ever mentioned leg action to me or indeed my lack of it, which on reflection was very strange. Ben Hogan, Sam Snead and all the great players in America at this time were available to discuss ideas on the practice ground. In England it was never like that. Nobody talked to anyone.

In England there was a reticence about helping or asking for help which remains today. It is amazing to me that so few young professionals have ever come up and asked me to look over their swing or if I would give an opinion. Maybe they thought I would not take kindly to that sort of thing—but if so they were wrong. Maybe I should have taken a sharper interest in them and approached them more often but it is sometimes difficult to interfere, indeed far more prudent not to do or say anything until asked as far as technique or style is concerned. As a matter of fact, I have never done a lot of teaching but I might start down in Spain on an exclusive basis—charging a lot! The point is that you do not get as good as I was at golf without knowing what makes the swing work. What I have learned over the years I have learned from other people and then put into practice myself. In the past ten years my swing has stood up magnificently . . . I just wish my putting had, but that is another story. I am not saying I know everything, but I do know a great deal and what I know I learned from the best—that surely gives me solid teaching qualifications and I find no difficulty in expressing myself in easily understood language.

Because of Bolt and Weiskopf I had the chance of playing with many of the top golfers who otherwise would have been out of bounds for a young Englishman like me. We played with Ken Venturi and Jackie Burke, later to captain the Ryder Cup team, and Ben Hogan. In fact I played the last round with Hogan before he quit the tour. It was final-practice day at Oaklands Hills in Tulsa. The temperature was over 107°F. It was a sauna bath. Hogan played all right but he was troubled by an injured knee and pulled out the next day, after which he did not come back on tour. He was always a bit distant and I never dared ask him anything about my game. I must say I found it extraordinary the degree to which the Americans held Ben Hogan in esteem because as far as I was concerned he went around putting people down, and enjoying it. Why, I've no idea. He had an incredible career, and made a courageous recovery from a car smash that all but killed him.

Hogan was undoubtedly a legend but by no stretch of the imagination could I ever class him as a nice man. He was not a warm individual and yet the respect he had at the Ryder Cup in 1967 for instance was awesome. When he walked into the team room his side stood up, including Arnold Palmer, Gay Brewer, Bob Rosberg and Billy Casper. I could not see why any man should gain that amount of respect. I could not understand why they wanted to treat him like a god. We don't hero worship people in Britain the way they do in the States. We specialise in knocking people down instead of building them up. In America they love heroes—think how revered the late John Wayne and Bing Crosby were or how highly Bob Hope, Palmer, Nicklaus, Sam Snead, are regarded. But Hogan seemed to get more preferential treatment than anyone I've ever met. It was at that 1967 Ryder Cup that Arnold

Palmer asked whether the American team would be playing the large or small ball. 'Who said you were playing tomorrow?' was Hogan's cold response, cutting Palmer down to size. It seemed unnecessarily sharp to me. I certainly did not walk in awe of him though I respected what he had done. I've met far greater men and women than Ben Hogan—like the Queen, who made me feel so much at home when I was invited to join a small dinner party at the Palace. Hogan enjoyed the aura around him, and enjoyed being talked about for his sneering remarks, like his response to Gary Player when Player phoned him in Buenos Aires for the answer to a query about the back swing. 'What clubs do you play?' Hogan asked Player, who had taken six hours to get through (the phone system was not as good then as it is now). When Gary answered Dunlop, Hogan replied tersely on the crackly line, 'Phone Mr Dunlop and ask him what you should do', and hung up, no doubt chuckling at how clever he had been. I just never saw the sense in that behaviour and never will.

My friendship with Weiskopf and Yancey also helped me to be accepted by the Americans, who have a certain mistrust of foreigners. Not Jack Nicklaus, of course, or Johnny Miller or Tom Watson—the top players don't mind, but some of those average fellows languishing halfway down or in the bottom half of the money list resent foreigners playing their tour and snapping up what they believe is their cash. Trevino was great and I have no complaints about Palmer, although he is not nearly as warm as Jack Nicklaus. That might surprise you because Jack has the reputation of being very cold and distant. I never found this but then I had a reasonably special arrangement with him in the early days. He was a close friend of Deane Beman who earned his US Tour card at the same school as I attended in 1967 and we were buddies too. Beman, a former amateur champion, is now Commissioner of the 16 million dollar US Tour. At the school that week Beman and I went and visited Nicklaus several times—the course we played was not far from North Palm Beach where the Golden Bear now has his headquarters. As a result of that and subsequent meetings I did a lot of fishing with Jack.

Basically over there all you do is keep yourself to yourself as much as possible and try to get on with everyone, although it was difficult to like—for instance—Gardner Dickinson, Howie Johnson or Bob Goalby. They have closed minds. They think nothing happens outside America, or they did then. They must have been flabbergasted when I took the American title from under their noses in 1970. The Americans are a remarkably insular race. I remember Dave Hill once standing up at a US Tour committee meeting and strongly making the point that he felt no foreigners should ever be allowed to play on the US Tour—and I was sitting next to him. I never tackled him about his opinions but at least I knew where he stood and I knew there were a lot more behind him with the same sentiments. Every player who has enjoyed success is realistic enough to know that not all American golfers resent international players becoming involved on the US Tour. On the contrary, they see international players adding considerable prestige to the Tour. The majority do not have tunnel vision, but then it is their broad-minded attitude which helps make them great. I have never met anyone at the top worldwide who has a closed mind—in fact the opposite is the case with the top stars and officials like Joe Black of the PGA, Deane Beman of the US Tour or Joe Dey, who used to run the Tour and is a former captain of the Royal and Ancient Golf Club of St Andrews. It is the lesser lights who foster the resentment. Severiano Ballesteros felt this undercurrent, too, when he first went over, and did not like it. Now he has been so successful he is made for life over there, but I bet the sniping will go on, especially as he has chosen not to make his permanent home in America. That at least would give the smallminded on the US Tour reasonable grounds for suspecting that 'the foreigner' intends to settle down in their country. It is a gesture of faith on the part of the incomer. Nick Faldo is doing that and he is fortunate, too, in liking the States as a place to live. For most of us it is a place to get away from quickly. When I was a youngster America was at the end of the golfing rainbow, a paradise to be sought after hungrily! Dreams can be rudely shattered, or maybe it is just that I'm getting older and my standards have changed.

As a new boy, of course, I was given no playing privileges, but it was easier for overseas players to join the tour then. I earned my ticket at the same school as Peter Townsend, former PGA captain and now highly successful professional at Portmarnock, and Bobby Cole, the former amateur champion from South Africa whose experiences in America so shattered his confidence. He plays around the world these days or accompanies his wife, the delightful Laura Baugh Cole, when she is playing on the women's circuit. Lack of success in the States also affected Townsend, who took many years to recover his poise. Another school member the year I got my ticket was Clive Clark who, surprisingly perhaps, gave up the plum job of professional at Sunningdale, but who now works for the BBC as their man on the ground and for CBS as an analyst at a handful of events. If they all found it difficult to cope with America I did not—initially at any rate.

In 1968 I became the first British winner of a tournament in America when I won the Jacksonville Open—a tournament I was to win again four years later, although on a different course. The first year I won we played at Deerwood. When I arrived in America that year I had cockily predicted I would win and had been shouted down by a local journalist. The press man was the first to come and congratulate me when I collected my first prize cheque in Jacksonville a few months later.

3
Settling In

With Vivien in the late '60s travelling around the States was easy. The country has a fabulous air network and the hotels were of a standard we did not know then in Britain. Every room had a private bathroom! No wonder the top Americans, until ten years ago, hated coming to Open championships at venues with inferior facilities like Lytham or Hoylake, Muirfield or Carnoustie. No wonder Sam Snead called coming to Britain 'camping out' when he travelled here in 1946 to win the Open and 1953 for the Ryder Cup! I got so involved in American life that I even changed the way I talked. Not deliberately, of course, but it did help me to get on with everybody. I couldn't help it really. I have analysed why it happened and I believe it was just an effort on my part to be more readily accepted. Peter Oosterhuis never changed but then he benefited for years from being the only Englishman on tour and made a lot of extra money as a result. He would have been daft to change his accent. He is as English-sounding today as he was the day he left Dulwich College, even if he is totally American in attitude and every other respect. Nowadays he hardly ever plays in Britain.

As for me, it helped, of course, having Vivien. I would not have gone to America on my own. I would not have done it—it is that simple. I would have been too lonely—I'm not a loner and could not go two weeks on my own. I don't like crowds but I do like having a few people around. I like to have company for dinner. I mean it—if I had not got married I might never have gone to America. That may be difficult to believe but it is the truth. Had I remained single, who knows what might have happened to me. I might have fallen into the trap of being satisfied in the late '60s with what was on offer in Britain. Success in life is not just wanting enough, you must want more and more. You can't afford to be satisfied. The road to success can be a long one and in some cases it is never ending, but I am sure that getting married put me well and truly on the right road. All of a sudden I wanted to be more and more successful, to buy Vivien nice things, to buy a home. It meant a change of lifestyle for me, but it was an essential change and one I accepted readily.

I had been living out of a suitcase, living in motel after motel. I was a golfing gypsy, sleeping here tonight, there the next, and returning from time to time to Mrs Baker's. Maybe I realised even then that I was never meant to live like that. You can go punchy, like a boxer who has had one fight too many, if you stay too long on the road on your own. Getting married meant being on the tour was far more pleasant, with Vivien along, but also meant I had to try harder—much harder—for us. We would stay near major shopping centres so that I had something to do if I was bored at the hotel. I learned my lesson quickly, giving those hotels situated just off freeways in the middle of nowhere a miss. They were prisons. There was just nothing to do if you did not have your own car to provide a means of getting away. We used courtesy cars a lot, and had no way of escaping in the evenings. It was awful.

I had practised a lot in the early days as a pro, finding out if this technique or that would work for me, and if it did I worked even harder to get to the point where it became second nature, where under pressure I never even needed to think about it. Having cracked it of course I eased off practising, though frankly I would feel guilty about this. After a round I would head back to the hotel while my colleagues hit pail after pail of balls. It seemed to me as if I was lazy, but I had discovered the technique and it was simply a question of keeping it well oiled. All the other fellows hammering balls hour after hour were still looking for the secret that would bring success. At one point I felt so uneasy about not needing to practise as hard as some of my tour colleagues that I started to join them for sessions just for something to do, but the more I practised the worse I became. That may sound like an excuse for not working on my game but honestly I did not need to. I was not being lazy, despite what some people thought. I had not let the good life get to me. Johnny Miller has had to cope with the same type of criticism after saying he knew his swing so well he could analyse where he went wrong on any one day and correct it in his mind's eye just sitting in an armchair.

Some people say I never worked as hard as I should have to sort out my putting problems, that my lack of form latterly was because I did not bother to practise the way I had once and that by easing up I contributed to my own decline, but that is rubbish. I was never, even at my peak, a great one for practice. Once I learned how to do it properly I did not enjoy practising—it seemed a waste of time. In fact the more I practised the more detrimental I felt it was to my game and whatever anybody else thinks I knew best of all what was good for me and what was positively harmful. People tend to think that practice means bleeding hands and hours and hours of punishing work. I used to play until my hands were sore and blistered when I was a kid but not as a pro and I never ever felt that I was not 100 per cent ready when I went to the first tee on the first day. I know people will say that isn't what it looked like when I played in such and such an event at such and such a venue but I honestly never, as far as I was concerned, teed up unprepared. My problem anyway was not physical or technical but mental and I'll grant that sometimes I may not have been mentally ready, although such was the nature of my problem that I was not aware of it. I will not accept criticism that I did not practise hard enough. Not everybody needs to batter balls all day to keep swinging well or keep his game in the sharpest order. Bobby Locke in his heyday would hit six or seven wedges and then go out and win the Open. He was never criticised and neither was I when I was winning but then when I wasn't people started looking for reasons why I was no longer on top and it is easy to cite a lazy attitude as an explanation.

All this practice lark started with Hogan, the iron man with an incredible devotion to the game—a total fanatical devotion—and with South Africa's Gary Player who has always been a demon for practising. Curiously the harder and longer he practises the worse his long game becomes and the more he has to rely on his fantastic short game, yet I often hear him say, even today, 'the harder I practise the better I become'. Poppycock . . . and I have told him so. Gary may sometimes have problems with his long game but he is a genius with the wedge and putter. It is his short game that often gets him out of trouble after he has hooked off the tee. He will never change and there is no doubt his impact on the game has been incredible—as staggering as his enthusiasm for it. No one, and I mean no one, has travelled further to win more major titles around the world than Gary, who likes to ponder what Jack Nicklaus might have been able to achieve if he had had to spend so much time in aeroplanes in the days before jumbo jets when it took ten hours to cross the Atlantic from London to New York, never mind the hours to fly from Johannesburg, where Player lived, to Washington. He is a golfing phenomenon who might, like me, have wished he had been born American to have taken full benefit of his undoubted talent. Yet I don't know either. He is so fiercely patriotic for South Africa, so committed to his country, that I doubt he would admit that, even if he secretly felt it.

It is not necessarily the people who work hardest at golf who do the best, despite what my parents used to tell me. There is little use working hard to perfect a swing that has basic deficiencies because you will only have wasted your time. A faulty basic technique will always let you down. One of the saddest things about golf is that once you have come through the difficult learning process, conquered the mental aspect, mastered the technique, you have lost some of the enthusiasm you had as a younger man. Sad to say, I suppose there is hardly any pleasure for me any more in ripping a ball 250 yds straight down the middle off the tee because it doesn't mean a thing! I know my problems, if there are to be any, will crop up when I get on to the green. In the old days, when I did not drive as long and as straight as I have done latterly in my career, there was the fun of getting out of trouble, but there is none of that now. The freshness, alertness and determination has all evaporated somewhat. Now I only get mad at myself when I play badly—but I'll be trying hard enough at the Open for the next few years.

Beyond a certain level in golf, putting is far more than 50 per cent of the game. Each tournament in America is a putting contest. It is the same in Japan and to a certain extent in Europe, although the inconsistency of the greens here makes putting far more of a lottery than on the other two circuits. Most of the better players in America hit most greens in regulation and whether they win or not depends—quite simply—on how well they putt allied to how badly their opponents do. But back to me.

I was always very fit at school. I was always top in PT and PE and was naturally very strong and I've been lucky with my health. I have had few injuries to speak of during my career, and have never needed to hang upside down the way Lee Trevino or Severiano Ballesteros have had to do because of back troubles. Of course I have a good swing which, because I use my legs properly, takes a lot of strain off my back. If you are using your arms a lot, you are putting a big strain on the lower back. A great many pros put far too much strain on their backs because of the way they swing the club. I know it seems daft that they don't change their style to ease their problem but it may well be they simply cannot do so. Having gone on so long with the same style the muscles are all well trained and a massive retraining would not only be a lengthy process but a costly one. So they make do as best they can. I was fortunate that I started with a good grip. I may not have bought an instructional book until I was 20 but I did read magazines and knew what a good grip should be. It is, in my view, a grip which is not too strong because, unlike Henry Cotton, I do not think the hands should play too important a part in the swing. In fact there are few of Henry's theories I do agree with, great man that he is. I interlock like Jack Nicklaus does because I am convinced that it is the best way. I used to overlap the little fingers of both hands instead of interlocking them but changed because I found myself closing the club face on the back swing as I took the club away from the ball.

When I linked both hands together I found I could execute a better take-away and get myself into a much squarer position at the top. Curiously I overlapped when I won my two majors, but remember that all through that period my tempo and timing were the key to my success. If I had a problem it was that I either pulled or pushed shots, for the simple reason that the club face was slightly closed at the top. My rhythm and timing had to be spot on to keep me straight down the middle. The switch I made, and the reason I made it, seem awfully simple now. A lot of these things are simple but it is knowing about them at the right time that's important. I found the best way to ensure you were gripping correctly was to put both hands on the club in a neutral position. If you lay the club head-down square to target and put the hands on palm to palm then close them then that's the grip. Interlocking is best – take my word for it, especially if you do not have strong hands, and most amateurs do not. When I decided to change my grip in 1974 it did not change my swing at all. All it did was help me line the club head up properly at the top of the back swing, something that then eradicated the fears I had of hooking and pulling. I effectively eliminated the negative thought that I might hit the ball left; I removed one of the worries I had lived with for several years. When you can eliminate the anxiety about the quick hook you are halfway home. The result of my grip switch meant my long game improved tremendously.

Sadly my putting began to deteriorate because the closer I was able to hit the ball to the hole, and the more birdie chances I set up for myself with my improved form, the more pressure I put on my putting. It's a vicious circle. I was always a great checker and re-checker of my swing. I would check it in my mind every day standing over the ball and going through the complete routine. I would check my grip and stance and that I was aiming properly—aiming where I meant to hit it. And I would check I had the ball correctly positioned.

Ninety per cent of amateur golfers and a fair percentage of the less successful professionals get two things wrong more than anything else–alignment and ball position. When I fix my aim I do not pick a spot a few inches ahead of the ball and in direct line with the target like Nicklaus does. I just make sure I'm pointing everything the right way. You soon

learn the correct way. I said to somebody the other day that
before driving off he should lay a club across his toes and
step back to see whether he was aiming where he really
wanted to go. He said he'd feel a fool doing that, but you can
be sure nine out of ten people get that bit wrong, and then
wonder why their balls fly off into the rough. That is one
problem that is easily remedied but it is a problem too few
people take time to check. The other problem is that people
play the ball either much too far forward or much too far
back in their stance. They don't work on a consistency of
position for every shot. The ball should be played from the
same position all the time whether you are using woods or
irons. Keep the game as simple as you can. I know some
people say that the ball should be moved backwards and
forwards depending on the club that is being hit, steep face
or shallow, but that's all wrong. I believe that changes the
whole pattern of your golf swing and that it alters your
weight distribution every time. That's crazy logic.

I have always been intrigued by swings. At Scunthorpe
as an eleven-year-old I would sit looking out of the lounge
window way down the eighteenth towards the tee 380yd
away, and I could recognise everybody as they came to
play by the way they swung the club, because basically they
always swung the same way. The only thing that ever
varied in their game was the position of the ball at address,
and if it was wrong (even slightly wrong) they did not play as
well as they could. Ball position is vitally important—I
cannot stress that enough. I worked it all out on the practice
tee and latterly, as I said, did not need to practise as hard as
others on tour. The only features of the game I enjoyed
practising were bunker shots and a few chips. Long-shot
practising was a waste of energy. Have you ever noticed
how little practising the golfers who are playing well do?
The leader of a tournament prior to the last round will get
out and warm up with a few shots, hit a few practice putts
and he is off. He is happy with his method that week and I
was happy with mine most of the time. How did I know?
Simply enough. If, as I did, I kept shooting low rounds I had
to be doing something right. I had no reason to query my
technique any more. Right through the bag I was well

satisfied with my game, but I never had a favourite club—one I enjoyed hitting more than any other—because I always felt that if I had a favourite there would have to be a club in the bag I liked hitting least of all, which would have been incredibly negative. I have always been a very positive person and quickly attracted the interest of those who make their living out of managing sportsmen.

I had joined the Mark McCormack organisation in 1967 after having had an exploratory call earlier that year from George Blumberg, his great friend in South Africa. George is on the International Management Group board and has exerted considerable influence on the affairs of the multi-million dollar empire, which was just beginning to expand when I came along.

I was happy to join the organisation, because I had twice nearly come a cropper. I had one manager who arranged for me to do a Mannikin cigar advert in which I hit a ball—a ping pong ball—off a table. Every time it flashed on the screens I received a royalty of 22s 6d. When I joined McCormack the other manager claimed that I had broken the contract I had signed with him and demanded £5,000 compensation. He had never done anything other than get me the cigar advert and I felt no responsibility to him at all but he persevered. Letters went backwards and forwards and it was becoming quite a *cause célèbre* as we came up to the 1969 Open at Lytham. McCormack's men, who are hard bargainers, might not give up so easily these days, but they decided then that I should pay and clear my mind of the problem before the Open. I was not completely convinced but realised the value of getting the matter resolved, so I paid him £5,000—£750 more than my winning cheque at Lytham the following month. In fact had we held out we might never have needed to pay. Two weeks after I sent off the cheque the fellow died and a week after that his wife committed suicide!

Then there was 'Pop' Pettit, an 80-year-old who approached me in 1967 about playing in the Canadian Open. I did not have the funds to go to Canada at that time but Pettit paid my fare on the understanding that I would pay him back. He was closely involved in the running of the

Canadian championship and I did reasonably well, finishing fifth or sixth and winning $4,000. This enabled me to pay off my debt and pay Pettit's expenses as well. That was fine, but then he was everywhere. I could not get rid of him and I found myself paying some of his bills. I was remarkably naïve in those days before McCormack came along.

Pettit had been involved with several other golfers, including the Australian lady golfer Margie Masters, but I was unhappy with his continual presence and told him I was joining McCormack and did not wish to have anything more to do with him. He was very annoyed and said he would sue for $10,000 but he had no leg to stand on. We had signed nothing at any time. He never sued.

The first knowledge I had of McCormack's interest was that call from Mr Blumberg. Not that he mentioned Mark's name. He just asked if anyone was representing me and said he felt I was going to have a marvellous international career. In such circumstances I needed a solid managerial set-up to cope with all the extras that would come along—extra engagements that involved time, effort and anxiety, when one already had enough on one's mind trying to win tournaments. Later I was asked along to the McCormack office in London for talks and I signed up.

At that time McCormack had Arnold Palmer, Jack Nicklaus and Gary Player, who formed the modern Big Three of golf, Doug Sanders and Bob Charles. Peter Townsend went there a month before me but McCormack had no other British clients. It is funny when I hear him say today that Michael Parkinson was his first signing in this country. He conveniently forgets Townsend and me. He always took 20 per cent but that was never a bad deal as far as I was concerned. I reckoned that 20 per cent of what McCormack could negotiate for me still left a hefty cheque in my account. Lee Trevino has been skinned twice by bad managers—he has lost fortunes estimated at several millions—but I have never had any problems with the McCormack organisation on that score. They are always totally straight. They have integrity—if McCormack says he will do something, he does it. Maybe he is not liked in some quarters but if he makes a promise he'll follow through. I have no complaints at all about the financial side of the operation. I have known Mark a long time yet I would not consider him a friend, rather a respected business acquaintance. He is a difficult man to get to know for two reasons. He never stops long enough for you to find out what he is really like—and even when you do pin him down, his mind is never far away from business matters.

He is a workaholic whose empire now stretches the length and breadth of the world. He has offices in London, Buenos Aires, Hong Kong, Paris, Melbourne, and several in America, with branch offices in half a dozen other countries. He utilises every possible second of working time—even to the extent that when he flies in to London in the early hours, he has his secretary meet him in the car so that he can dictate memos and notes on the way to his breakfast appointment. From the modest beginnings when he saw the potential of managing Arnold Palmer (now a multi-million dollar earner every year because of his many shrewd investments in real estate property and the like) McCormack has made a veritable fortune out of golf—but at a cost. A few years ago he needed a major operation to relieve pressure on the brain, which should have forced him to slow up—but it has not. He really is something else, an incredible entrepreneur.

4
Triumph at Lytham

George Blumberg and Mark McCormack expected me to do well and I did—maybe even sooner than they thought. I was a very mature 24-year-old when I won at Lytham. I think a lot of that came from having played in my younger days with older men. County golf involved a much older set than me and I learned a lot. I think that was an important factor. I even married an older woman—Viv is a year older than me. All these things meant that I was a little older than my age in terms of experience.

After winning Jacksonville in 1968 I played the Open that year and shot 79 in the last round at Carnoustie to finish sixteenth. I just was not ready to win. I was confident enough to feel I could but it was not until the following year that it all came right for me. I remember I tried to play each day at Lytham as it came, the best way I could. Obviously the great thing in any event, but most importantly the Open, is to get off to a good start, and I did with an opening 68. I was in the hunt from the first day. It was easier to cope with the Open in those days. There was not the razzmatazz there is today and I had toughened myself mentally to try to handle the pressures I knew I would face. Given the chance of winning I felt sure I could take it. I tried to act as normally as I could all week. It was easier to do that then. The whole atmosphere of the Open now makes it more difficult for a British player to cope. Of course I was psyched up. I would have been kidding myself if I had thought I could treat the actual championship as just another tournament. Of course I couldn't. I always knew how important it was but where the kiddology came in was on a shot-to-shot basis. Come on, I'd say to myself, you have played this shot a thousand times before! As I lined up for a difficult approach I'd talk myself through it and I was never in doubt that I could win. I just forced myself not to think about it! That would have broken my concentration—and it is the ability to shut out everything around, all the distractions, and focus the mind firmly on the job in hand that separates the ordinary golfer from the real champion.

I think I have always been a big-occasion man, inspired rather than frightened by the applause—some people are frightened by it. It always gave me a good feeling (even if it did increase the pressure) to hear so many people cheering for me. It was great when I was playing well—but not at all satisfying when I wasn't, when I knew what they were expecting of me and knew I could not produce it. At these times, the crowd were positive in their support of me but I was negative in my whole approach. But in 1969 I had no worries!

Playing and winning in America at Jacksonville had sharpened up my game and of course I had won previously on Lytham. During Open week the wind blew strongly from the west and to do well you needed to make the turn in 33 or better. I did. It so happens I enjoy playing in the wind because I have always enjoyed manufacturing shots and that was what I had to do that week. It is a question of compromising on every shot, often—in Britain—in a howling gale, like the one that hit us at Turnberry during the 1973 autumn equinox! At the Open in July 1969 it was just breezy—not strong enough to cause the Americans any problems. Our winds in Britain are much heavier than anything the golfers face in the States. I have had to struggle to control my delight when watching even a good American star closing the face on a 7-iron for a 140yd shot into the wind here in Britain when I know a 5-iron hit like a long chip is best. The shorter the time the ball is in the air, after all, the less likely it is to be affected by the wind. We all have our yardages for different clubs in our bags—167yd for a 6-iron, for instance, in my case—but when the wind blows textbook play gets blown away too and a golfer must rely on feel and touch.

Lee Trevino is the past master of these manufactured shots, Christy O'Connor Senior was a brilliant exponent, Chi Chi Rodriguez from Puerto Rico was no slouch and

45

today we have that master of the distinctively personal shot—Severiano Ballesteros. To be honest you either have or haven't got the ability to play these shots. You cannot learn the skill; it is inside you. I know I had it and maybe it was because I had to play golf with make-do clubs for so long as a teenager. Seve Ballesteros, Chi Chi, Lee and I all used improvised clubs in the early days which were not tailor-made for us, far from it. We had to think of ways of using the clubs as best we could to get the ball in the hole. We were forced to experiment. Golfers who began playing seriously with fully matched sets, and who have never been forced to try playing a variety of shots with just the one club, lose out! Mind you, there are many different ways to play, suiting different types of personality. All ways achieve the same end and ultimately it is down to mentality to sift out the stars from the average golfers. When we go down to Nigeria I spot a great many youngsters with very special talent but sadly with nowhere to play. They have one event a year and during a break in the tournament our caddies and half-boys—the lads who carry round the drinks as we are playing in the broiling sun on the sandy courses—scratch out a hole in the ground and start playing with makeshift clubs. They hit incredible shots from horrid lies in the dry dirt and sand not far from the putting brown—the mixture of oil and sand used as greens in Nigeria. Unhappily all they ever get to do is carry someone else's bag or the tray of drinks—it seems so much talent wasted because they can play all the shots.

I hoped I could play all the shots required of me at Lytham in 1969—and did. My main—indeed my only—problem was keeping my mind on the task in hand. I have a vivid imagination at times and I found myself thinking much more vividly that week than ever before. I was way ahead of myself. I could see myself with the trophy yet I knew that it would be easy to whip a ball over a fence out of bounds or run up a 7 or do something stupid on the last day, which would shatter the dream. I had shot 68, 70 and 70 and concentrated hard all the way round on the final day, just trying to swing smoothly. Then on the last hole New Zealand's Bob Charles drove and said he thought his ball had gone into a bunker. I knew bloody well it had not. I had seen it skip through and past because I just happened to watch his shot very carefully. He was my only real challenger! I don't know whether he genuinely did not see where it went or whether it was a little bit of gamesmanship on his part, but I knew where it was and I went on to win by 2 shots on 270 with a closing 72.

I felt great walking down the last and a surge of pride swept over me when the ball dropped into the cup on the green in front of the famous old clubhouse and I knew it was over. The impact hit me much later although we did not celebrate lavishly. We did not go and get drunk on champagne, but had a quiet dinner with family and friends and it was the following day that I'll admit I felt a change in myself. There seemed to be a new-found confidence. The achievement had made me an even more mature competitor. I had always had the belief in myself, that I could do it, but it is only when you realise your dream, when you achieve the status you have been aiming at all your life, that something happens inside. The accumulation of all the time and effort I had expended on reaching my goal, plus that new-found confidence, gave me a heck of a feeling of pride. When I put my head on the pillow that night knowing what I had achieved, I felt prouder than I had walking on to the last green that afternoon! I was very well satisfied. I had reached the top of my pinnacle—the one I had started to climb ten years earlier in Scunthorpe. I did not think then that it would be the first of many—I simply wanted to enjoy what I had at last achieved.

I did not, however, get much time to enjoy it. Within hours I was off to America to play in an event I did not want to play in, before huge crowds who did not appreciate what I had done the week before. At Westchester there was no hero's welcome—I was just a name on a draw sheet. I was drained but I wanted the emotion of the moment at Lytham, the excitement of the achievement, to linger on and on and on. I wanted to savour it, but I never really got the chance. If you have given that much of yourself to achieve something that few people do in their careers it should be given more than one day's acclaim, but I had charged back to America where a victory story only lasts 24 hours before the previews are being written for the next event.

For my parents who had encouraged me a lot my winning the Open was a great moment too. A great deal had happened to me since my mother caddied for me in the Lincolnshire Open when I won. They were happy enough in those days that I was interested in golf but they never realised what was going to happen to me. We were just an ordinary family. My father once took me down from Scunthorpe to play in the Carris Trophy but most of the time I travelled with friends on the team. My folks after all were not in a financial position to help very much. After my win at Lytham I could afford to treat them!

Ultimately it is easier for an American player to come to Britain and do a hit-and-run job on the Open because the pressures on him are not the same. He knows the championship is the greatest in the world, that it gives him recognition round the world that he might never have hoped for or expected, but for any American the big one is the US Open—his national championship. Winning our Open gives an American considerably more up-front credibility as an international star but given the choice of winning only one of the titles he would always plump for the US Open. For British golfers the British Open is the really big one, the championship that, were he to win, would guarantee him a million pounds, probably more than a million these days. The implications, the rewards, of winning are so great that the pressure imposed on British players at Open time are now huge. It is the same in tennis. We have done better in golf, with home wins from Fred Daly (1947), Henry Cotton (1948), Max Faulkner (1951), and myself in 1969, than they have at Wimbledon where Fred Perry was the last British male tennis player to win, way back in 1935! All right, talent comes into it, of course, but the pressure does not make it any easier for us to win at home—it makes it a hell of a lot more difficult.

There was a million-dollar tag on winning the Open when I was successful sixteen years ago, so just think of the rewards that would be lined up for a home winner of the title

Above: Me aged three with my sister Lynn, who has never really been interested in golf. Now that she lives with her family in Spain near us she might take it up! *Sunday Express*

Left: On holiday in Mablethorpe when I was interested in playing with a much bigger ball. My mother is pushing Lynn in the pram while my grandmother looks after me. . . and I don't seem too amused. *Sunday Express*

Top: The first trophy I ever won — the Lincolnshire Boys' (under nineteen) Cup. I was thirteen at the time. *Sunday Express*

Above: That strong-looking inside left is me in the school team aged about fourteen (second left). I got injured too often in soccer and decided to concentrate on golf — and I am glad I did. *Sunday Express*

Top: Not too many husbands are allowed to take their golf clubs with them on honeymoon — I even took mine to my wedding! Viv, who has always been more than considerate, had a go with an iron. *Daily Express*

Above: This is how it all began for Jacklin in the States in 1968 at the pre-qualifying school with (left to right) Peter Townsend, Clive Clark and Bobby Cole. Rapt attention from the others but it's all a bit of a bore for me — or so it seems. *Clark's Photography*

Above: Johnny Rubens, who helped me so much in the early days at Potters Bar, was on the spot when I came home with the Greater Jacksonville Open trophy in 1968.

Right: I beat Lee Trevino on this occasion at Wentworth in 1968, but he beat me in the big one — the Open four years later. We have always got on well — even if he does talk a bit too much on the course!
United Press International

The joy — and the anguish! — of my British Open victory at Royal Lytham and St Anne's in 1969. *Associated Sports Photography*

Top: Prime Minister Harold Wilson discusses golf and tennis with the 1969 *Daily Express* Sportsman and Sportswoman of the Year: yours truly and Ann Jones. *S & G Press Agency*

Above: After I won the US Open a victory cavalcade through Scunthorpe was organised for me. Not quite a New York-style ticker-tape welcome but a great, great moment in my life. *Daily Express*

now. It could be many, many years however before a British player takes the title again. When I took the title they had only just moved away from chalking the scores up from time to time on a blackboard in the press-room. Today the Open is bigger than ever, the fields are stronger than ever, and the pressures on home golfers from a huge partisan crowd are mind-bending. If a British golfer wins the title he will have had to cope with many more distractions because of increased media attention, and also he will have found it more difficult to concentrate with so many more people around.

I won and I was as good as I had to be at the time, and that's all that matters. It is one of the reasons why it is impossible to compare golfers from different eras. Who is to say whether James Braid, playing with the equipment he was used to, was a better or worse player than Ben Hogan, or whether Harry Vardon was better than Walter Hagen, was better than Henry Cotton, was better than Arnold Palmer? It is not even all that easy to compare Nicklaus and Watson, so great have been the changes in the game, the improvements in equipment. You can argue all night about that in the pub. All I'm saying is that I'd be delighted if a British player should win the Open and experience what I experienced in 1969, but to do so he will need to be a very tough competitor to cope with the dozens of new distractions. I'd be delighted, of course, but in a very small way I'd be only too well aware that I really was getting older, that I had dropped back a rung or two in Open history, losing my tag as the last British player to have taken the title—a reputation I have enjoyed for sixteen years.

I certainly would not feel any resentment if one of the new young men of golf took the title, just a feeling of pride in British golf again. Every year it comes round I wonder if this is going to be the year I lose one of the feathers in my cap. I have seen Faldo and how well he putts, and have been incredibly impressed by how he has coped with the pressure. He is our most experienced challenger at the moment because he has been in contention for the title and knows already what pressure can do to his silky touch on the greens. Trying to put yourself into a cocoon of concentration is the most difficult thing in the world for a golfer to do, and trying to do it at the Open, where you know you just have to be at your very best and not let chances go abegging or make costly silly mistakes, takes a very special iron will. A British player's best chance of winning will come if he manages to get five or six shots clear of the field, then does not let his imagination run away with him on the final day.

I was in a position to win the title five years in a row and managed to win it just once. Nicklaus, the greatest golfer of all time in my book, has been in contention almost every year since he started coming in 1962, and he has won only three times. He has had to make do with second place seven times and third three times and he is, as Muhammad Ali would say, 'the greatest'.

Nick was unfortunate that he met Tom Watson on his best form at Royal Birkdale in 1983, just as Watson was unshakeable at Muirfield in 1981 when Ken Brown challenged but found the pressure appallingly difficult to handle. In 1969, the year I took the title, I was fortunate. On the final day nobody made a move at me. I shot a reasonably mediocre 72 and pulled it off. If somebody had come through on the final day sixteen years ago with a 65 in Tom Watson style (remember what he did to Nicklaus at Turnberry in 1977), I might never have won. The numbers that are produced at the Open now are incredible and no British golfer today will have the luxury of winning without having to fight every inch of the way. That does not mean to say that if Faldo, Sandy Lyle, or Sam Torrance move four clear with a round to go they will handle themselves with other than considerable credit, but it will not be enough to shoot par to win, not these days. Remember there is not only the American threat to the British challenge, but there are golfers like Greg Norman from Australia, Seve Ballesteros from Spain, Bernhard Langer from West Germany, all in there trying their damnedest to win, without having to face the pressures a British golfer has to face in front of his own folk in his national champion-ship. The inspiration is there for a British player to win the title—the massive rewards are on the table for all to see but that inspiration only puts a British golfer with the ability in a position to win, and then pressure takes over to make that task the hardest in golf.

I should have had a couple of weeks off to enjoy my Lytham win but I never got the chance, I never gave myself the chance. My main aim of course initially was to become the best player in the world and I suppose for a fleeting moment I was when I held both the US and British titles. I wanted to be even better than Jack Nicklaus but things did not work out quite that way. I realised I could never achieve it when I decided to quit America full time, when I took the decision not to move permanently to America. What helped me make up my mind was the fact that I knew all the big money deals were sewn up in America by Palmer, Nicklaus and Trevino. The opportunities for me over there were limited—after I won the US Open in 1970 I made little or no money in the States on a contracts basis. I became disenchanted with the States but fortunately, the expanding European Tour meant there was money for me on this side of the Atlantic. I played for years over here in Britain with a guarantee of £2,000 just for showing up. I knew I could make a lot more in prize money in the States but becoming part of the hollow society over there did not suit me, and so I stayed in Britain, effectively giving up the battle to be the undisputed world's No. 1.

The problem was, having decided to stay here, England was not big enough to cope with a really big superstar. I was not left alone long enough to live a reasonable life. I was hounded by the press. It came ironically to the point that the only time I had any respite was when I made a short trip back to the States and became almost an unknown again. Daft that—because when we had lived for six months in America Viv and I longed to get back home just to see some English trees or eat some good old English vegetables. I'd long to do a spot of shooting again for pheasant, absent on almost every US menu. In short, although America became a bolt hole to escape to from time to time, we preferred the superior English way of life and I think we did right in hindsight, I have few regrets.

It is curious, on reflection, that I never bought a place in America, although I very nearly had an apartment at the classy Sea Island resort in South Carolina for a time. I had signed a contract with them after winning the Jacksonville Open for the first time and things were going well until I won the Open at Lytham and that bumped up my contract fee. Then I went and won the US Open and my manager Mark McCormack asked for $150,000 and a duplex apartment overlooking the lake. Sea Island just could not afford it. We came close to a settlement but in the end there was no agreement.

5
Necessary Qualities

It is always difficult, even with hindsight, to assess how good a player I really was when I was at my best, but I was aware that I had exceptional talent. The one disadvantage I had was that I was not born American. I always felt it would have been easier for me to make use of my talents had I been an American, and been able to cash in on their massive deals and contracts. I don't want to appear unpatriotic about this of course—but any golfer wanting to reach the top does have an advantage if he happens to be a citizen of the country which has the largest, most competitive Tour in the world! In just the same way an American who happened to be an above-average soccer player might regret being American. (Soccer is very much a minority sport over there.) That American might wish he had been born in Britain or Italy or Spain, where footballers are capable of commanding huge salaries. Anyway I am not American—I am British, and proud to be.

I never did make any money out of being the US Open champion. Over there companies did not want to know me—the Englishman with the funny accent. Nice as some of the Americans I met were (and hospitable too), I never really felt in the slightest bit at home there. Maybe it was the welcome I got from some of the players! I am very sensitive to atmosphere and situations. I can remember once I played with Bob Goalby, the uncle of the Ryder Cup player Jay Haas, and he never spoke a word to me all day—not one word. He did not say 'Hallo', just handed me my card, never commented on any shot I hit, and did not say goodbye. He had no reason to dislike me. I guess the game had just got to him—golf does that you know. I had to accept his weird behaviour. I spoke to him and did my own thing, but it was like playing with a ghost or a robot!

Another difficult person to play with was Steve Reid, who used to roll over on the fairway when he got mad or played hockey with the ball around the hole when he was having trouble on the greens. He just could not take failure. He was such a perfectionist that as soon as things went wrong he lost his head. Tom Weiskopf was like that, which was a shame because he was such a good player. Tommy Bolt quit more tournaments, it was said, than he actually finished. Not true, of course, but he did pull out of a good few during his career.

In Britain there are not so many golfers who cannot cope but there are more than you might think just managing to and no more. Ken Brown had problems at one stage in his career but he has reformed, and Brian Barnes, always an extrovert showman who sometimes went over the top, is cutting back on his golf tournament appearances—just like me. It's a tough game which can send a guy round the bend if the mental pressure becomes too great.

My father, as I said earlier, was never the most generous of men as far as pocket money was concerned, to either myself or my sister as kids, but then he probably did not have too much left over from the day-to-day running costs. He has—and I think he would freely admit it—a mean streak in him as far as money is concerned, but although on the golf course it helps to have a percentage of meanness in your approach I don't think I do. My father has taught me, however, the value of money—of having it, of saving it, of using it wisely. In a way I don't think he has been able to enjoy himself as much as he might have because his outlook has inhibited him all the time. It's easy for me to talk like that, however, now that I live in a style to which I am growing more and more accustomed the older I get. It was a struggle for my folks to make ends meet and keep up standards, and I never forget that.

Although I may not have a competitive mean streak on the golf course I did learn early how unwise it is to give the other chap a chance. I was about fifteen and playing in a County match against a real nice fellow. I was one up and eased up and he beat me by a hole. I never consciously eased up in a match again—indeed I do not find it easy to play other than full-out now, whether in a tournament or in a bounce game with friends. I never play these days without keeping a score and I always play to win because I know of no other way to play. If I learned anything as a kid that helped me later to become a champion it was that to be a successful golfer you have to be a disciplined person. I am totally disciplined now even in my normal lifestyle, controlling my drinking to a social evening glass of wine and a liqueur, smoking only very occasionally—I could and have given up completely from time to time—and running my life with a certain precision.

I like to be organised, to know what I am doing, where I am going, what the arrangements are. I am a meticulous time-keeper, having never ever come close to missing a tee-off time in my life. I could not possibly have survived on tour the way some of my colleagues do, travelling hopefully. Some of them arrive at the venue with minimal luggage and then try to fix up a hotel—all far too relaxed and casual for me. Discipline, ability obviously, and a desire to be the best are what drove me to an Open victory. I just always wanted to be the best. I cannot take second best and I hated it when I lost form in the late '70s and was no longer a force to be reckoned with. The desire to reach the top was part of my character. I have always felt that the goodies are life's winners and the goodies are those who work hard to achieve their success. I am a great romantic too—a dreamer who always imagined himself walking down the last hole and sinking the putt to win the Open. When it happened for real it took some time to sink in that the dream had become a reality, but having achieved my dream, I suppose there was a certain anticlimax—the feeling amateur actors and actresses feel after working hard to put on a play successfully, then suddenly finding it is all over. I used to stand in the wings of the Scunthorpe theatre watching my mother—who was and still is a very good singer—performing in amateur musicals, and I sensed the feeling of elation after a successful show and yet disappointment when a production closed. If I had not been a golfer I think I would have loved to have been a singer—holding audiences in raptures singing hit songs.

Mind you, I would not have wanted to be a down-the-bill performer. I would have wanted to be a star, singing the same songs year in year out and getting marvellous acclaim for it. I enjoy adulation up to a point and would enjoy the attention that top singers get—with selfish reservations because the more famous you become the more you have to work hard to protect your personal life. The shine of being easily recognised quickly wears off. As a lad I used to know the words of hundreds of songs. I was great on lyrics, a great fan of Elvis Presley and could reel off the words of all his ballads. I loved going to the cinema, especially to see musicals and, if they were romantic, I'd get misty-eyed about it. A *Rocky*-type film would have had an incredible impact on me had there been that sort of film around. Indeed the Ben Hogan life-story *Follow the Sun*, in which Glenn Ford played Hogan, had the effect of strengthening my resolve to become a successful tour player. I loved that. I saw myself more in Hogan's role than as an Elvis Presley. I saw the film several times. Hogan himself hit all the shots with Ford, of course, featuring in the close-ups. It was made in black and white, but perhaps one day the new techniques will be used to bring it to the screens in full colour. It was a great film.

When Viv and I got married I told her that we would have everything later on—servants, big cars, big houses—and we have. I remember she laughed all those years ago and I did too, but I had set my mind on winning the Open, and once you've done that, I believe there is nothing you cannot achieve given a modicum of luck along the way and reasonable help offered from time to time by people who know you mean business. It's easy to tell when someone is serious about something, and nobody could have had any doubts about my intentions. It was an intense passion of mine, and people knew that I was in earnest. They knew I meant business when I talked of clutching the famous Open cup—the cup played for since 1872, when young Tom Morris took the title after making the original championship belt his own property by winning it three years in a row from 1868. There was no Open in 1871 because there was no belt to play for—it was on young Tom's sideboard up in St

Andrews—but then the cup was produced for annual competition and the three-years-a-winner-and-its-yours rule was deleted, which was just as well because Jamie Anderson won three times in a row from 1877, Bob Ferguson three consecutive years from 1880 and, in more recent times, Peter Thomason of Australia in 1954, 1955 and 1956—just three of his five wins.

Some of my golfing colleagues are history freaks, reading all about golf, collecting for their libraries and constantly mooching around antique shops looking for old clubs that can be worth a fortune to dealers in America, but I'm not big on that. I don't think much about the past—the present is all right, but I think more about the future, although I must admit to feeling a surge of pride when I won that cup in 1969, the cup won in the past by the 'greats' Harry Vardon, J. H. Taylor, Ben Hogan, Walter Hagen, Henry Cotton, Sam Snead, Bobby Locke, Thomson Palmer, and Player and Nicklaus. For one whole year it was mine and my name is on it for ever.

I could never have won if I had not had an inner strength of purpose, and the sometimes selfish independence of spirit to go and do my own thing to achieve it. I had a fair amount of independence at home so was used from an early age to taking decisions, even if it was about daft things, like whether to eat my mother's jam tarts or not. That was the start of my being careful about what I eat. I may have been a little overweight as a youngster—I had a very healthy appetite—but that puppy fat soon disappeared when I moved into my teens. To get to the top I knew I needed to be fit and I knew I couldn't get as fit as I wanted if I ate jam tarts, so I didn't. I never take sweets or desserts: I'm careful about my diet.

On the course I was disciplined enough, when I was trying something different, to give it a real try, not chop and change to the point where I was confused and was not sure what was making me play better. My whole life was disciplined because that was the way I wanted it to be. Although my first set of clubs were old and battered and tatty-looking they were all I could afford, and I cleaned them and polished them and made them look a million dollars, just as I did with my first car—a real old banger. It was an Austin A30, which I spent hours polishing and repainting. It was not all that good a car but it was mine and it had to look and work perfectly or I was not happy. From about the age of thirteen or fourteen I bought my own clothes and shoes, which always had to be gleaming. Once at Royal Mid Surrey I was wiping a pair of shoes down with an old towel before going out and a fellow went by and laughed. 'Nobody will worry about your shoes, nobody will notice them,' he shouted, but even if they didn't I knew I would notice. I was always very finicky about these things, still am in fact. There is no room for sloppiness anywhere in life.

That finickiness came, I am sure, from my parents. My dad was always careful. He came from a very poor family background. He was one of a large family and as a boy he never had anything new. A biscuit was a rare treat for the kids. I remember years ago visiting my grandfather in a house which had a dry loo in the yard serviced by the dilly man. When they eventually got a toilet with a chain and full flush, that was real progress. From that kind of background, where money was very tight, it is hardly surprising that my father has never been one to take a gamble. He is much too cautious, has far too much respect for the money in his pocket. I gamble but even then only after considerable deliberation.

My mother came from a totally different background. Her father hardly ever worked. He was invalided out of the First World War but I never knew what was wrong with him. To me he always looked fit as a fiddle, and he lived to be 87. He had a ladies outfitter's shop.

I knew that to have any chance of being successful I had to have the right temperament, and this is something that you have to be born with. If it is not there naturally it is a heck of a strain keeping your temperament in control, staying cool, calm and collected. As it is, I am a reasonably easygoing guy but that is misleading. It camouflages just what a worrier I am. If I have an 8 o'clock starting time I'll go to bed the night before at 9 o'clock, just to get a full eight hours' sleep—I need that. But I'll be wide awake by 5 o'clock, just to make sure I don't miss the alarm. That's the kind of thing that niggles, worries, causes me unease.

I worry too about things I may not feel I am in total control of. For instance, Peter Alliss and I were once signed up to do a double act at a night club in Stoke-on-Trent—nothing so grand as the London Palladium, where before the Second World War Henry Cotton used to do a stage act! We had the star spot and were scheduled to do a golf routine, except that half an hour before we were scheduled to go on we did not know what shape the act would take or what we would do. That worried me—especially as there were 600 people waiting to see us. Peter sorted it out in his own relaxed way. He decided he would do a bit about me and that I would talk a bit about him lacing the conversation with a joke or two. It went off all right—I think—but we were never asked anywhere else. It was all fairly nerve-racking, having been paid up-front to produce the goods. It was not really my scene although I quite enjoyed it when I got out on stage. Maybe the waiting was the bit I hated most, just as I used to hate waiting all day for my tee-off time if I was going on in the mid-afternoon in a major championship. At Lytham in 1969, Viv, who was expecting Bradley at the time, and I went off in the car to visit some old historic castle or ancestral home not far away just for something to do. At the US Open I played all day with Bradley taking my mind off the golf as much as possible. I've often wished I had Jack Nicklaus's knack of taking an extra long lie-in, but I'm far too active-minded to just turn over, relax and have another couple of hours. He is very lucky.

In addition, Nicklaus more than anyone realised what his human limitations were. He more than anyone else I have ever known knew just what his capabilities were in terms of how much of himself he could give or had to give to achieve his goals. And nothing swayed him from his schedule. There are many places in America where the name Nicklaus is not popular—Greensboro in North Carolina, for instance, because he just never plays there. It is always staged the week before the Masters at Augusta and Jack's priority is to be at Augusta for practice. He always prepared so meticulously in the early days for championships that it would never have entered his head to go to Greensboro, and he probably never will now.

Nicklaus is also fortunate in being better than anyone I know at utilising his nervous energy in the proper way. Every golfer has nerves, just as every stage actor has. We and they would be worried if we did not because it is an indication that the adrenalin is flowing through your veins. It means you are keyed up for a performance and we golfers have to psych ourselves up too in the hope of producing a low round. I believe that the first three holes of any round are important in helping you get that nervous energy under control. Once you have got into the swing of the round, and started to play, your nervousness tends to disappear—or you become less conscious of it because you are having to concentrate so hard on the business of making pars and birdies. If you think hard enough you will not have time to be nervous. I remember when Eddie Polland, that live-wire Ulsterman, won the Spanish Open at Valencia in 1980, I could see in his eyes he was going to win, despite the fact that I was trying as hard as I could to land the title. Polland did win because that week nothing was bothering him. He sat quietly on a bench when there were hold-ups, when normally he might have been expected to jump around in an agitated way. Nothing put him off that week. His level of concentration and control of his emotions were such that he was almost in a trance. I've experienced that. It's marvellous.

When I started out with my aims and goals I knew that just being a good player would not be enough to make me a big-time winner, an international success. I needed to be a great deal better than good, and I knew that meant branching out, doing my own thing and not being one of the boys, a member of a group. I knew I had to be my own man, just as in the past Neil Coles, Eric Brown, Dai Rees, Ken Bousfield and Christy O'Connor had been. They were all independent spirits, never caught up in the plans of others unless they wanted to be. Being single-minded and independent did not mean being stand-offish or anything like that—it just meant getting on with the job and not caring if sometimes you were not popular with the others. I was not seeking popularity first and foremost. I wanted to be a winner, and I knew I could not do it as a member of a gang. I had to do it on my own.

6
On the Treadmill

In 1970 I was playing very well and was full of confidence going into the British Open, especially having won the US title just a few weeks earlier. I was very 'up' in 1970 and the creditable start I made at St Andrews—eight under after ten holes—reflected the mood I was in. Then the rains came. Just as I was about to hit my second at the fourteenth hole it came on really heavy. Somebody shouted out as I was on the backswing and my concentration was broken. I did not swing properly and the ball ended up in a bush. People often say that my chances of winning that year were written off in that moment, but in fact I was still in contention in the closing stages of the last round. I missed a short putt on the sixteenth—a putt I felt I had to hole to maintain my hopes of retaining the title. I missed from 2ft. On the last green I missed again, this time from 8ft, which would have tied me third, but finishing fifth in defence of my title was not bad.

What might have happened had the weather not intervened is only conjecture, but I was in Britain as the US champion and I think a lot of people expected to see a new Jacklin. They did in one respect at any rate—if anything I was more sure of myself than ever. Well, could you blame me? Success in golf is all tied up with a player's state of mind and that state of mind can be improved so much by boosted confidence which in turn is the result of major wins. The more you win, the more you are capable of coping with the knocks the game throws at you. It's a hell of a game! Just when you think you have got it beaten it turns round and hits you hard, sometimes below the belt. Jack Nicklaus was right—it is not a fair game and never has been, but it is a great one. Bad breaks or indifferent performances affect golfers so adversely that you have to learn to handle disappointment, you have to work at ensuring all negative thoughts are dispelled as quickly as they crop up—and that's sometimes not as easy as you think if everything seems to be running against you.

When you are playing well then you never give anything a second thought. It's all so enjoyable and you win if you putt well. Putting is the easiest thing in the world to do but the circumstances surrounding it make putting difficult and those circumstances are sometimes dependent on a player's mental attitude. It is vitally important to have total concentration. I concentrated exceptionally well when I won both Opens but I did not have total concentration—that happened only very, very occasionally in my career. It is possible to put yourself in a cocoon of concentration. I've experienced that but not as often as you might think, and I certainly had to work hard to do it. It was not something that happened easily and naturally. I don't know why it happened when it did, why I should find it so easy one day to concentrate and then have to wait a year until I felt the same way again. If I knew how, I'd have done it every week and I bet I would have won a lot more often.

There are stringent controls on golfing equipment to ensure that we cannot hit the ball further and further and make golf courses obsolete but there are no controls on the mental aspect of the game, which in my belief is 95 per cent of golf. There is great room for experiment and eventual improvement of performance, experiment that would have helped me, perhaps, when I landed in so much trouble with my putting. I tried so much to sort out things in the conventional way. I tried not looking at the ball when I hit the putt because I had got myself into such a mental twist about hitting it. I tried to adopt a could-not-care-less attitude, to the point where I was trying to convince myself that it did not matter whether I holed or not but I couldn't fool myself. I still missed. It was crazy. After all I was the positive-thinking cocky young lad who had won two major championships. The simple reason for my problems—and I see it now as clear as ABC—was that I pushed myself too hard after my two big successes—pushed so hard that I did not want to play any more. It was a mental reaction. It was the equivalent of the tyres burning out in a car or an engine overheating and causing a breakdown—only in my case I didn't stop. The danger signs were there quite clearly in my inability to putt, but I was driving on so furiously I did not see them. I never gave myself the chance to sit quietly in a room and ponder the problem. I never, at that point in my career, ten years into it just after 1973, gave myself the time to think out logically what had happened to me.

Nothing changes the cycle of nature. It just goes on and on at the same leisurely pace, but we rush around at our own hell-bent pace creating mental problems for ourselves. I can look back now and understand exactly what went wrong. I was an average normal lad from an average normal background and environment who took up golf seriously because I happened to enjoy it. And I enjoyed it when I wanted to enjoy it, I was in control. Then all of a sudden after my two major wins I found myself not in control any more. Other people decided where I should play, or suggested where I should. Situations were thrust upon me, and because of the financial rewards and the circumstances—I had become such a good player—it was impossible to turn them down. I could not say 'no'. It was not my fault that the game had expanded so much that there was somewhere to play in the world every week of the year, with over 40 events at that time in America alone instead of 20 as there had been not many years earlier. It was not my fault that there were over 20 European tour events (mostly British in those days) instead of the dozen of a few years earlier. Times were changing, golf was booming in Europe, and I was in at the ground floor taking full advantage of the bargains on offer, never realising the effect non-stop action was going to have on my game later.

It was not natural for me to play almost every week—I had not done that even as a boy. I had often taken a few weeks off when I got bored with my form because I was playing poorly. I never got a chance to collect my thoughts. Gradually, very gradually, I built up to a breaking-point at which stage I really did not care whether I played or not. People laughed and thought I was joking. The offers still came and I did not help myself. I did not refuse them when I know now I should have. It seemed for a time as if I had gone off my rocker, I was in such a dazed mental condition. I pushed myself not for a few months but for a few years because the money was good. I never knew what a good schedule was. Every year I tried to sit down and write one out, one with built-in breaks, but I'd always get it wrong.

I'd pick ten events to play in not because I liked the people or the course or fancied the prestige of the title: I played because the sponsors were offering the largest prize money and something extra on the top for me. I failed to pace myself properly—I played when I would have been better resting, and didn't play when I was reasonably fresh because the sponsor was not offering the appearance incentive. I got it all wrong. I never had a quiet year. A couple of times I tried to be sensible but generally I was stupid. I started in 1968 and I just played on and on and on until I was completely shattered. Idiotic—but I was being driven on by the huge financial carrot dangling in front of my nose. I was the donkey. Of course when I was making a name for myself, I inevitably wanted to play. Having made it with the two big ones I did not realise the importance of pacing myself properly. When I was in the States I played every week because a week off in the same hotel that you would have stayed in if you played anyway seemed pointless. That was the hard thing over there. With hindsight, it would have helped to have had the benefit of an American home to slip back to from time to time, a place where I could for a short spell anyway escape the pressures of the US Tour. Instead, in the early '70s I burned myself out and paid the penalty later on the putting greens of Europe.

Other players have different metabolisms and can cope. I couldn't because I abused the game and the playing of it so that it only gave me disappointment and distress. I pushed myself too far. I was good in the first place because of me, I had achieved what I had because of me, not because of anyone else. I did it all on my own; I stole ideas; worked bloody hard; I made it myself. And then when I got there I started listening to everything that was talked and written about me. I was the subject of discussion in locker rooms, in the papers, on television, in the streets. I was being compared week after week to other golfers; I was the subject of in-depth analyses—why was I not doing as well as some of the other players, some even older than me—Jack Nicklaus, Gary Player, Arnold Palmer? It all added to the pressure I was already feeling because of my crowded schedule.

I got to the stage where I stopped reading the papers for fear of what I might read next. The plain fact was that talent had rocketed me to the top—I'm not immodest on that score, you have to be talented to win the Open—and money was the motivating force behind everything I did and everything I did was under the public and media microscopes. Maybe it would have all been different if I had come from a totally different type of background, from a wealthy one where money was less of a fixation. Nicklaus has never had any money worries in his life, not as a child, or as a teenager and certainly not as a highly successful golfer—the world's greatest golfer. Fifteen years ago he could afford to turn down $60,000 appearance money when they wanted him in Japan. I'm busy, he would tell them or, I'm doing other things that week. I would have gone if I had been offered a deal far less lucrative than that, simply because it was too good to pass up.

They said that winning the Open was worth a million dollars to the British golfer who achieved it and I wanted to be that million-dollar man. I wanted the money—and made it, but then did not realise what the—let's face it—blind pursuit of money was going to do to me. You try to do your best for your family and your bank account and your golf, and in my early twenties I thought I knew everything. I didn't and it was all compounded by my trying to play regularly for a time on both sides of the Atlantic. I played the US Tour while trying to bring up a family in Europe and then I got involved too on the European circuit again, as John Jacobs began to build it up to what it is today. I was splitting myself three ways, trying to do my best on three fronts and burning myself out in the process. My wife Vivien urged me to slow down, but earning money, getting money in the bank, meant security for me and her and the family. That drove me on.

It always has been and always will be tough for foreigners in America. The American airline network is so efficient that golfers with a base there can whisk home on Sunday night at the end of a tournament and have a few days off. I could not so easily slip backwards and forwards across the Atlantic to my home, much though I would have loved to do it, it would have been far too costly and far too tiring. For Viv and me the schedule each year was a mess—and remember Viv was the first wife of an English pro to be full time on tour with her husband. Now a great many wives are on tour, but we were the first. I had been one of the first professionals to leave England and go overseas in the winter, although I never went on what was called the Cutty Sark tournament—I didn't know the right people then. Neil Coles went to America one year and hated it; Dave Thomas went and did not settle down; George Will went and I think could have settled there but his wife did not want to move; Peter Townsend went and it was tough for of him; Clive Clark went for a time, then came back and won a tournament only to quickly tire of the tedium of on-tour play. He switched to far more lucrative avenues. Now he is one of my colleagues on BBC's television team so we join forces again.

Townsend was far more promising than I was when we both went to get our US Tour cards, but unhappily America shattered his confidence. He suffered for so long from that dreaded disease of golf, the shank. Brian Barnes would have done well in the States with his power game but for personal reasons he too preferred to stay at home. Mind you it is very easy to look at the world today and think it was always the way it is now. In fact when we all had a go at the US Tour it was still taking us twelve hours to travel to New York on strato-cruiser or Pan-Am clipper. Jumbo jets only came into use in 1969—sixteen years on they are still one of the greatest planes ever produced.

During the period 1967-73, when I was most successful, and won the US Open, I never found winning easy. In fact, even allowing for Hazeltine where it all seemed to click so wonderfully, I was nervous and up-tight about the possibility of failure at the last hurdle, although I tried not to show it, tried to act very normally. I was nervous about winning in Scandinavia in 1974, when I took the title by thirteen shots. I remember going to bed the night before the final round wondering about the possibility of taking 80 and losing. It meant of course that there was no complacency when I went out next day. You might think that that showed a negative aspect of my character, a character which was otherwise very positive, but I would rather consider my attitude realistic. I have seen fellows shoot 80 on the last day and lose. I knew this was not impossible if my putting let me down. That putting again—always the putting in the back of my mind to torment me. And it started to go wrong in the States.

The delight at my win in America was offset to some extent by the disillusionment of what America, the place I had long dreamed about, was really like. When I first went there everyone had been very friendly, but when I won a couple of events fellow competitors just walked by—not the top stars of course, but the middle-of-the-money-order men, the fellows struggling to survive, who definitely felt I was taking money out of their pockets. Of course I had flown in to their country and I was doing just that. If nothing else at Hazeltine I did have the satisfaction of putting two fingers up at the miserable fellows on the US Tour—guys like Dave Hill or Howie Johnson, whose comment to me after I won the US Open was not 'Congratulations' but a surly 'You holed some putts'. I told him he was right but that I could have missed a bunch of them and still won. He was typical of the group who felt that the American Tour was for Americans only. Happily Deane Beman has helped to make it more international although his brief, I'm sure, is to keep making it as difficult as possible for interlopers to move in from overseas.

I always went out of my way when I was in America to be extra nice because I was a visitor there and I thought I needed all the friends I could get, but the mentality of some of the players over there was incredible—you cannot imagine how many head cases there are on tour. The game has driven them potty. The pressure has got too much for them. When they cannot take it, bitterness takes over.

Their attitude becomes twisted, distorted. I know what I'm talking about because three years ago I was beginning to experience that kind of aggravation. While fortunately not becoming totally overcome by it, I was annoyed that I could not do what I used to be able to do without thinking—especially on the greens.

The week I won the US Open I got a putting tip from Bert Yancey's brother Jim. I was playing great but, surprise surprise, my putting was not worth a damn. He said that one way of sorting it out might be to look at the hole as I putted rather than the ball. It seemed a novel idea. I tried it on the practice ground, found it worked and also that it gave me a new positive feeling in my hands because you had to follow through to the hole. I putted like a dream. Indeed it is the best I ever putted. I had always been a streaky putter, and as time went on I had realised that while I was sometimes quite brilliant most of the time I putted like an 8 handicapper. I tried to relax myself by being partially hypnotised before the round but ended up frustrated by my failure to hole out when I got on the course. I even went to Ron Hubbard's scientology courses to see if they could help me find a more positive attitude. We got the answer (Viv also attended the course) and ran before they could get their claws into us. It was simple psychology. I would sit in a room with a scientologist who would ask me what my problem was. I told him putting. He asked me what part of putting I couldn't face and I said I couldn't actually face anything. He just underlined to me that I was thinking negatively and always had about putting. It was just worse now as the tensions of being at the top had begun to take their toll. I was never really my own man. I had commitments here, there and everywhere. Of course I was making big money, but at what cost? I was on a crazy merry-go-round I could not get off, a roundabout which seemed to be getting faster and faster. I was caught.

I remember as a youngster when I played too much and started missing eight-footers I would opt out for a week or two, even for a month, and come back fresh and eager. I was playing 30 to 35 tournaments a year and as the pressure mounted I started missing more and more medium-length putts until I lost all confidence, but I could not take a break. I was committed right, left and centre. Almost every year, as I began my build-up for the Open, McCormack would come up with a wonderful deal. For instance, in 1970, the year I was defending my title at St Andrews, I filmed around and after the Open an eighteen-hole match with Arnold Palmer—a project that necessitated my getting up at 6 o'clock in the morning. My instinct was to say no, but the fee was $10,000—far more than the first prize in the Open. I found it tough to refuse. I enjoyed being the top British golfer of the time, and the excitement of the sideline contracts it generated, but to handle all that you have to be fresh, young and eager, and it helps if you happen to be rich. I think the biggest drawback I had was never having had any money—I could not get the earning capacity into perspective. I believe, as I said, that had I come from a rich background I might have found it easier to turn down $10,000 deals, but if I had come from a rich background I might never have won an Open, because my attitude would have been totally different. I was never forced to do anything. McCormack's men never rang me up and said I had to do this, I must do that. I always had the option of saying no. Tragically I said yes far too often. No was an obsolete word in my vocabulary for a number of years and I paid for that omission.

There was another important issue that affected my thinking. I was living in the wrong place. I was living in England and paying taxes on everything I made here, which was fair. I would never complain about that, but by the time the Wilson government came in I should have been off to Jersey or the Isle of Man——anywhere to try and protect my wealth. The one thing I wanted more than anything else from the British Open was security for me and my family. I had enough brains to know that people with money could do everything they wanted. It did not bring happiness but it helped a lot. I never thought about Jersey because I was too busy playing golf. Staying in Britain for several years longer than I should have cost me a fortune. This is where I lost out.

7
Contracts – Good and Bad

Whatever a golfer earns as a result of his performances on the course—and remember that the top Americans these days are earning in the region of half a million dollars a year—it is possible to make two or three times that amount in business contracts. Golf attracts a great many internationally known sponsors aiming their advertising at a quality market through golf, and some of the deals that are being struck these days are staggering. Severiano Ballesteros can command huge fees for advertising top products, but then he is highly marketable! Not only is he a top sportsman with a worldwide reputation for excellence; he also happens to look incredibly handsome. Whether he is advertising knitwear, men's toiletries or even a well-known credit card he benefits from having a macho Spanish appearance which sends most women crazy. His looks are as important to him in an earning capacity as his golf but he would not be in a position to use his looks if he were not a winner worldwide.

The scope these days for international contracts is greater than ever, and if there is one thing I regret it is that Mark McCormack's organisation did not do a very good job of selling me outside the golf world. What I have always believed is that I needed a major non-golfing product to keep my name firmly in the news. Remember how long Denis Compton maintained his association with Brylcreem and look how well Henry Cooper has done. I have never been promoted in that way and frankly I think I should have been. I have a great deal to thank the McCormack Organisation for but they seldom got me the kind of deals I was really looking for—those which did not involve too much active participation from me.

The organisation has never been all that strong on

coping with other than specific contracts tied in closely to the sport in which their client is involved. In my case this meant that every deal struck on my behalf required me to be somewhere at a given time to do a certain thing. It was tremendously restricting—most times pleasurable but frequently (I am being honest with myself) it was quite inconvenient. Yet I had the answer in my own hands—I could have refused and did not do so, which is why I can hardly now be ultra-critical of the Mark McCormack team. That is all in the past now—at 41 I just feel I have not enjoyed the exploitation my name deserved. It may all come in the next 20 years.

The scope in all my new golf-related ventures in Spain may make more money for me in the long run than my performance as a player. It is curious that one of the best contracts I ever signed was the very first major one I was offered. This was the one with Pan-Am in which I was contracted to fly backwards and forwards across the Atlantic in what in 1969 was the new jumbo jet—the 747 we all take so much for granted now. It was worth $37,000 a year for me for four years, 1969-72, and I hardly did anything in return for the money. The company forgot about me, or did not know how to use me.

My first golfing contract, of course, was with the Dunlop company. It was logical that it would be because Bill Shankland was a Dunlop man when I went to work for him. As mentioned earlier, it was Dunlop who gave me my first matched set of clubs. It was Dunlop who supplied me as a young assistant with new golf balls, although I recall them being handed out like gold dust. It was Dunlop who signed me up, initially for £100 a year, and I stayed with the company a long time—too long as it turned out. They signed me up on a ten-year contract. It sounded good at the time because it was signed before Britain got caught up in roaring inflation. There was no indication in the late '60s that we might get caught up in an oil crisis that would change the whole pattern of living and doing business as we knew it. At the time I was delighted to have the long-term security, but later the Dunlop contract became an aggravation and eventually I bought myself out—something no golfer had done before. It was the only thing to do in the circumstances because Dunlop refused to negotiate a new deal which took inflation into account. Latterly my association with Dunlop became very unpleasant but things had been going wrong for quite some time. In the late '60s and early '70s they were an ultra-conservative company and frankly I could not understand why they did not adopt the more go-ahead approach in business of their American sister company or the Far East operation. The company were just never willing to have a go with a new product. They were all nice enough chaps but everyone seemed scared of the man above him. I was as upset about the set-up at Dunlop as they were when I bought myself out.

The sort of thing which used to annoy me with Dunlop was their attitude to the model of club they marketed under my name. It was a good seller and every year I used to go up to Glasgow, where they had their factory at that time, to meet the staff, tour the factory and more specifically make comments on my club model. It took me three visits to realise that no one was taking a bit of notice and that the venture was simply seen by them as a PR exercise. They just were not listening to what I was suggesting they should do. For instance, on one occasion, having seen what was happening in America I suggested they round the face of my clubs a bit more. They said they could do it for me but not for the mass market. That seemed crazy to me. On another occasion I queried the colours that were being used to market the product. The old Haig Ultra was being sold at the time with a gold and black colour scheme which made the club not only look distinctive but very attractive on the shelves. Dunlop were using mauve, blue and white in combinations that did not gel. I asked them to give my clubs the new American look but they would not. The following year my clubs looked the same as always but their own Dunlop Maxfli model came out looking the way I had wanted mine to look. That made me see red and I had the McCormack Organisation stop the sale of my club—which I could do under the terms of my contract. There was a massive row, and the company's attitude was summed up by the then man in charge, David Sealy, who wrote me a letter pointing out that much though the company appreciated my views they preferred that I did not get involved in these matters. They knew better than me regarding the design and look of my clubs.

It was ridiculous but I was tied to them with this awful contract which was worth less and less to me each season because of inflation and the fixed nature of the deal. Finally I bought myself out with a year to go for £5,000. Finlay Pickin, the managing director, took the break-up badly and all but ignored me. It was silly really but I knew what was right for me and I had no conscience about getting out of the deal because I reckoned that the honourable procedure would have been to re-negotiate in the light of the economic situation. I was, after all, the former Open and US Open champion.

I had for some time also suspected that Dunlop were not playing ball with me. My contract involved a guaranteed sum of royalties on the sale of my clubs, but when enough Jacklin clubs had been sold to cover this annual fee, there was a distinct cooling off on the promotion of the clubs while the company started pushing the Maxfli model or the Peter Thomson clubs which had not done as well. In short I did not then, and never have, regretted leaving Dunlop for one minute. I like to work with go-ahead people. People who once in a while are prepared to take a chance—a chance that really is not such a gamble as all that if it has been carefully thought out. The company has changed now but the old Dunlop regime did not seem to bother too much. Even after winning the US Open title in 1970 I never had a contract with them that covered the United States. It seems daft, but it is true. They just did not appreciate the possibilities, or maybe it was their meanness shining through—the kind of meanness that prevented them re-negotiating my European contract and must have had the directors rubbing their hands in glee at their luck in getting me so cheap. None of their players involved with the British end did all that well. Graham Marsh, their key man in Australia, made plenty out of his Dunlop contracts only because he was dealing with the Japanese end of the operation, and you know how live-wire and switched on the Japanese are.

When I finally left Dunlop (and I had been playing other clubs but using a Dunlop bag to carry them in for some time, which I suppose was naughty) I was approached by the Ping company, whose founder Karsten Solheim was a personal friend of mine, and indeed my parents had got to know Karsten and his wife Louise very well too. There was a great deal written at the time about my switching from traditional-looking clubs to the Ping clubs with a revolutionary and—as far as some people were concerned—not too pleasant look about them. I have always said that any top player should be able to play with any kind of club but the switch was not actually all that dramatic. Ping arranged for me to have a set of their clubs designed to the same specification as my old Dunlop ones, with, very importantly, the same kind of shaft as I had been used to using. I am sure Karsten was not too happy about that but he accepted it even if he took a lot of persuading.

Karsten and I had a sort of soft spot for each other. We always got on well. I always spoke my mind to Karsten. I never buttered him up. I told him the truth as I saw it and that was what he was looking for—a candid opinion. He has had some marvellously successful ideas but they have not all worked. You could hardly expect to have a 100 per cent success ratio, although Karsten is such a perfectionist, thinks out projects so meticulously, that he probably has every right to consider failure as unthinkable. He is a great engineer and his product, produced in his marvellous factory in Phoenix, Arizona, is superb. It is hard to think that his multi-million-dollar empire began in his car garage just over 20 years ago. Some of his concepts, while magnificently workable in an engineering sense, do not always prove so effective from a golf point of view. Very light heads on very stiff shafts do not work, I venture to suggest, for most professionals although I think the combination works well for amateurs. Ping clubs also have a big head which gives an amateur more confidence that he is going to hit the ball properly. The consistency in the manufacture of Ping clubs is unique. They are incredibly strong, with a colour coding system designed to make it easier for an amateur to select the club most suited to his build. The colour code gives information on the angle of the head, and consequently how upright or otherwise a club is at address—something which it is important to know. A tall thin man requires a much more upright club than a tubby little fellow playing round his stomach!

All this is fine for amateurs, but the stiff-shafted light-headed club can tend to make the professional swing more quickly under pressure when the adrenalin begins to flow. At first I don't think Karsten was prepared to accept this and initially few professionals played them. Of those who did many were women. Over the years he has modified his line and been forced to manufacture clubs designed to the specifications of the professionals on his books. I would think he regrets this compromise but he is now far more likely to listen to constructive criticism than he was in the early days of the development of a range of clubs which have now been copied by other manufacturers all over the world, not least in Japan. Maybe I have made him more conscious of the golfing values as opposed to the engineering aspects of club design.

Karsten's company is the result of his trying in the early days to produce the perfect putter—the club that everyone would want to play. Of course it did not suit everyone—it couldn't—but the number of pros using one of the many models in the Ping range is remarkable. Just look out the next time you are at a tournament or are watching golf on television. Incidentally, the name Ping was chosen because when the ball was hit with the original putter produced by Karsten it pinged when it left the club head! I would say Karsten has made as much money out of the game as most people I know—except Jack Nicklaus and Arnold Palmer, although their earnings per annum make them tough men to beat. However, Karsten's golf business is now only slightly more than a quarter of the work he does in Arizona. His high-quality precision-tooling work is included on spacecraft and Challenger and Columbus missions. Indeed so much of the work he is involved in is secret that parts of his factory are high-security areas—no-go warehouses and machine shops. He is wealthy enough to have bought the club of which he was a member, named—appropriately for someone involved in providing some of the hardware and instrumentation for lunar missions—Moon Valley. And he has now bought his own course in this country too, not far from his English base at Gainsborough in Lincolnshire, my home county.

When I joined Ping it was not for a great basic annual salary but I was immediately involved in Karsten's exceptionally generous bonus scheme—one which rewards achievement through the year, assuming you have been using your Ping clubs of course. If you use woods, irons and putters you qualify for full bonus, with proportional pay-outs if you don't use the woods or leave out some of the irons in favour of a wedge or a 3-iron from another set. I was well treated by Karsten in some other ways too, but at the end of the first year of my exclusive contract I was very worried about my game and the way things were going with my golf in general. In desperation I resorted to my old set of Dunlop clubs for a couple of events and Karsten was not at all happy. I had played Ping all year but when I abandoned them his reaction was very quick. He did not pay me. I realised that I had broken the contract but I did not expect him to take such a strict line and at the time I was very upset. I thought he would have realised that I was at my wits' end and was trying anything to get my game back.

As far as he was concerned it was a black-and-white case. I had broken the contract and that was that. He would not even pay me a percentage of the £15,000 fee to cover the time I had used the clubs that year. He did not realise what I was going through mentally at that time, with all my putting problems, and that all I had been trying to do was make sure it was not the clubs that were wrong by going back to a set that I knew I had been successful with in the past. At that time Karsten was so wrapped up with the development of the Ping models that it was unthinkable to him that anyone contracted to him could act the way I did. Maybe I was to blame too for not having sought him out and explained the position. Maybe if I had laid it on the line he would have been more conciliatory but I suspect he would have been distressed to think that I thought there was something wrong with his precision models. The trouble was I needed to prove it to myself and on reflection I probably went the wrong way about it. You don't mess with Karsten Solheim and get away with it. Probably I knew deep down that he would argue very strongly that he had taken thousands of photographs of his clubs being tested—photographs taken down to millionths of a second to prove that the head did not move at impact and so on—but I was not interested in all that. I was not like his testing machine. I was a human being with problems of my own.

It was an anxious time but we never fell out so badly that we were not speaking. I may have been annoyed at his firm line but I was also realistic enough to realise that the trouble I had heaped on myself was really my own doing. What I had done by ditching the clubs publicly was not in the best interests of Ping, even if it suited me to do so at the time. Maybe I selfishly expected to get away with it but I should have known better. Maybe I was thinking so negatively at that time on every front that I was not thinking straight. Anyway I learned a lesson. Throughout 1974 I was getting into such a quandary about my golf that I wanted to try and get back to square one to see if I could pinpoint what was wrong. I did not realise the problem was in my mind. Karsten understands now, I think, what I was trying to do, even if he still would not agree with my actions regarding his clubs, but we have teamed up again to underline that if there were any hard feelings they have been forgotten.

I am now one of the Ping company's main golf-club testers on a consultancy basis. I play the clubs irregularly, it is true, on the circuit, because my appearances are limited, but I use them for company days and advertising purposes. He is happy and so am I because he is again looking after me very well and has agreed to make up Ping clubs to my own specification—D2 or D3 swing weight and not too stiff a shaft. They suit me very well indeed. The incident with Ping has passed, and I would vigorously deny any suggestion that I wanted out of the Ping contract in 1974 in order to sign up one of the most lucrative club deals ever with Spalding. That was just not the case.

When I was left again without a clubs contract, Spalding

came along and offered a deal I could not really refuse. That contract lasted for three years and the clubs were all right but not as good as the clubs the company made in the late '50s. In addition I did not have a happy relationship with the Spalding executive with whom I worked, but once again it was the money that finally sold me on the idea—£25,000 a year over three seasons, one of the best clubs contracts signed at that time. I knew of course that some people were saying that I was so keen on the monetary aspect that I would play any clubs if the financial deal was right, but I was not worried what people were saying. Nobody has played more clubs in his career than Gary Player and no one ever accused him of jumping on the gravy train. The point was that when the Spalding deal came along it was a time of depression when all manufacturing companies were suffering. The market was so saturated with clubs, many being shipped in from the Far East, that it was unusual to get such a good deal as the Spalding contract offered me. Most manufacturers could not afford to pay huge retainers. Mind you—and I say this with hand on heart—if I had thought that playing Spalding clubs would have adversely affected my winning capacity, such as it was at the time, I would not have played them and would not have signed the contract.

The manufacture of clubs has now gone about as far along the road as it can. Nothing really new has happened in design since 1965, allowing only for the Ping concept. Gimmickry has crept back into manufacture, but all today's gimmicks have been tried before years ago and been discounted—powerpoints, heel and toe weighting, speed slots are old hat. Every year, in this highly commercial world of golf, there has to be something different to improve sales. The average golfer is being conned—in the nicest possible way—by extra special packaging and by clever advertising and marketing. Look in any professional bag and you will find very few gimmick clubs—the woods are most likely persimmon headed just as they were in the old days. There might be the odd metalwood for fairway play, but basically the sets are standard design, tried and tested over the years. A great many amateurs, when buying clubs, go for something expensive and shiny, and manufacturers cater accordingly. The latest club I've been testing for Ping is a copper-headed club which is neither better nor worse than the normal variety. They retail at £80, but I am sure they will sell like hot cakes nonetheless—that is the nature of the game.

That is the story as far as clubs are concerned and the deals surrounding them. Balls are far less complicated or controversial an issue. I started with Dunlop because of my contracts made when I first joined Bill Shankland but in 1971 I changed to a ball made by the Ajay company in America and stamped with my name. I was on a bit of an ego trip. Ajay were into golf accessories but not clubs. I carried their bag and played their ball which they kept telling me showed up brilliantly against all others on the market. They showed me the results of tests and I naïvely believed them. In fact the ball performed in such an inconsistent manner as to be virtually useless. Not to put too fine a point on it, it was absolute rubbish. It was so inconsistent that I was really messed up by it, although again I was not sharp enough to realise this at first. Anyway I was concerned enough after a time to give some balls to friends on tour to test and they came up with the same report—the ball was no good. So I went to the manager of the company and told him that I honestly did not think the ball was any good. He sat back in his chair and told me that he did not think it was either. It never had been. I could have hit him right there and then I could have killed him on the spot. I had gone through a year of torture with that ball. At that point I took a decision. I would never again experiment with balls—it was all too risky. From that day I have played the Titleist simply because I have never had a bad one. The quality control at that factory must be out of this world. No suspect ones ever slip through. You can have total faith in a Titleist. The balls are so good that there is no need for the company to hunt out golf professionals to play them. The professionals would use them anyway.

Some of the best contracts I have had in my career were Japanese, and here I have to lavish praise on the McCormack men for their behind-the-scenes dealings which landed them for me. I still have some operating, including one for shirts. I remember at one point I received a cheque for royalties from the company concerned for $55,000. I thought there had been some mistake and sent the cheque back querying whether the computer had wrongly added on an extra nought. Back came the cheque with a covering note saying no one had made a mistake. I had contracts covering all manner of things in the Far East—sweaters, gloves, trousers. If I did well out there imagine what Arnold Palmer was raking in. Over ten to twelve years I have made not far short of £550,000 on Far East and Japanese contract deals with very little effort on my part—and this was all money which I am sure would not have been available to me without Mark's organisation. I still have my own set of clubs on sale in Japan—the Tony Jacklin model—but amazingly when I go and play in Japan (I haven't been there for two years) I do not even need to play them. The manufacturer knows I could not be expected to switch from my usual set for one week only, so has never even tried putting it in the contract. If they are happy so am I. It is still a very good club. I am endorsing the club, after all, even if I'm not using it—a fine point which emphasises the way golf is going these days. I had something to do with the original club design but nothing more. The manufacturers said they did not need any more help thank you very much—just like Dunlop. My own theory is that there should be far more co-operation and interchange of ideas between players, designers and manufacturers than there is.

8
Drama at Muirfield

In 1971 at Royal Birkdale if Lee Trevino had had a par at the last hole, Liang-Huan 'Mr Lu', the inscrutable Taiwanese golfer had birdied and I had eagled we would have tied. 'If' is a big word in life—and in golf too. As it was, Mr Lu hit a lady with a wildly hooked second shot from a grassy slope and knocked her out. (Fortunately, she made a good recovery and years later he took her on an all-expenses-paid trip to the Far East as compensation.) Despite obviously being shaken by the incident Lu took advantage of the luck he received when the ball ricocheted back off the lady's skull on to the fairway to make sure of a birdie—and of finishing a stroke clear of me. I birdied but so did Trevino, to finish winner by a shot, and in the process complete a unique treble in just five weeks—the US Open, the Canadian (one of the most prestigious of the tour events) and the British title. Little wonder he threw his jockey cap up in the air in delight. I doubt whether anyone has ever had such a magnificent three weeks.

I am sometimes asked why it was, if I was so good, I won only one Open. I'll tell you—people don't know how close I came each year. In 1968 a poor last round finished me but I was still in the top fifteen, I won in 1969, I was fifth in 1970, third in 1971 and third again in 1972—a reasonably good record I think you would agree. By 1972, when the championship returned to Muirfield, I was feeling really mature. I felt I had all the experience I needed, and when I came back to Scotland I had already won the Jacksonville Open again—on a different course, incidentally, from that on which I had won the title four years earlier. Winning my two majors was only made possible because I went to America and took on the best opposition each week, to toughen myself. I remember how upset I was when a newspaper headline said, after I won the Open in 1969, that I was now forgiven for leaving Britain. I don't forget headlines like that. I don't forget easily when it comes to idiotic statements like that by people who clearly had no conception of what I was trying to do and how I was going to achieve it.

That made me very angry but at the time there was still a considerable group of people who thought only of Britain and the Empire, who just did not understand that there was a big world outside where it was necessary for me to make the grade and prove myself. The reason we Europeans are catching up now is that we have players today who do understand that you need to become better in order to end up the best and to become better you need to play in ideal conditions against high-quality fields. If you are not going to make it to the top, then America will certainly find you out. The courses in America that the Tour visits are for the most part perfect in every respect. The greens roll well, unlike some in Europe where the ball can on occasion bump its way to the hole and (if you are lucky) drop in; the fairways ensure top-quality lies every time and you play mostly in ideal weather conditions. It's the best place to perfect a good swing technique, and once you have done that then you build up confidence, and confidence makes winning easier.

I remember vividly that when I played in the United States regularly some players would not go to Florida because they did not like the constant buffeting of the wind sweeping over what is essentially a flat uninteresting state. They felt the wind beat their swings to pieces—yet the wind down there is never anything like as strong or heavy as we can experience here in Britain. The opting out by even a few from the Florida segment was an indication of the excellence of the conditions expected week in week out. To be fair it is more difficult for us to provide the type of facility here that American players enjoy every week. Many of the courses are new developments, while here in Britain courses are hemmed in between houses most of the time with little room if any for a decent practice ground, a prerequisite at every American club. Jack Nicklaus's practice ground at Muirfield Village is so massive that you can hit full shots in any direction on the circular range.

We could do something about the condition of our courses at some venues—but not all. We could supervise the preparation of the courses more, but basically the European Tour is not always able to contact a club and start giving orders, even in the nicest, most diplomatic way. Those involved in the Tour are sometimes reticent to tell a club greenkeeper when it might be best to cut the fairways or which height might be preferable for the grass on the greens, yet we should. The sponsors pay heavily for the privilege of using a club. It is no reflection on the hardworking greenkeeper, who is often most used to preparing a course for heavy amateur weekend play, to offer him advice when a group of 144 professionals requiring higher standards than normal descend on his course. In fact I would reckon that nine times out of ten the club greenkeeper would welcome far more guidance. The fear is that if there are too many demands made on a club they may decide to opt out, and it is essential to keep the best clubs involved in the circuit happy. I would say that the standard generally of week-in-week-out venues has improved but we too often end up at courses of inferior standard. It would not happen in America, but there the Tour officials have far more power and—let's face it—there are hundreds more courses from which to choose. If you run into trouble with club officials there, you just move the tournament somewhere else where you are more welcome.

Today most clubs give the European Tour a tremendously warm welcome and enjoy the prestige that being a tour stop brings them, especially if the event is being televised. Hundreds more visitor green fees can be sold, benefiting the club coffers, after a course has been seen on television. What I would like to see is a uniformity in the condition of the courses we play in terms of the fairway length, the speed and texture of the greens and the pre-tournament procedure for irrigating and feeding the course. We are, I suspect, no closer to getting a uniform system in Europe than we were 25 years ago. Of course it would be much tougher to monitor than it is in America, but it should be done nevertheless, especially now that the Tour really is big business. I suggested twelve years ago that we needed to do this, and was instrumental in arranging a meeting with Tour venue greenkeepers at Wentworth. We talked a lot but I wonder how much it helped . . . very little I think. It may have been because there was a lack of money then to implement proposals but there is not such a shortage now.

The European PGA Tour is a successful operation financially but I wonder whether sometimes their priorities are wrong. Neil Coles once said to me he would play golf down a tarmac road if the money was right—and he is the chairman of the board. It is an incredible attitude—and one which highlights the difference between him and me. I wouldn't entertain such a thing. Most of the Tour committee men agree with Coles, so what chance is there of anybody changing anything? Thank heavens I have missed Monte Carlo both years—the event is played on the top of a mountain. The prize money is a generous £100,000 from Prince Rainier but had I been there in 1984, when the thick cloud on the top of the hill where the course is laid out meant the event being reduced to a ridiculous now-I-see-you-now-I-don't Feydeau farce, I could not have kept my mouth shut. The European Tour is booming. Prize money has doubled in three years to over £4 million, and I'm happy about that. I think the chaps are very fortunate to have sponsors putting up that amount. As for playing conditions, I was on the committee for ten years and often said what I felt on the matter but just got outvoted. That is why I got off. It was a question of trying to convince committee members, many of whom just did not think the way I did—and I failed.

Golf in Europe is sometimes the near equivalent of playing tennis on a bumpy court. In such unpredictable conditions you could never hope to become a world star. Once when I was on the committee Brian Huggett told me that it was all right for me to talk about what should be done when I had a Rolls-Royce sitting outside, but I pointed out that I got my Rolls because of the attitude I adopted. If you want things or believe in things badly enough you will go out and make them right or you end up second rate. The Tour is a respected organisation but it would gain even greater respect if it insisted all the time on nothing less than top quality. Frankly, being on the committee frustrated me. I would lie awake at night thinking about some of the decisions that we had taken until I decided enough was enough. I am no longer on the committee—indeed it would be difficult for me to attend meetings anyway now that I am based in Spain—and I honestly do not miss the involvement.

To return to 1972, that year I thought I was going to win the Open. What prevented my taking the title for the second time were some extraordinary circumstances over a two-day period. I played better golf that week than Lee Trevino, who had virtually given up hope of winning when he played his second shot at the seventeenth into a bunker. He had jacked it in—had honestly conceded in his own mind. He said so and it was not gamesmanship—we knew each other better than that. I had after all already had the incident in the World Match Play Championship where I told him that I did not intend getting involved in his lighthearted banter. He told me I did not need to contribute, just to listen, but I switched off and concentrated so hard round Wentworth on that occasion that I never heard half of what he said. He was chattering away as we came down the seventeenth at Muirfield but if he said anything to me directly I never heard it because I was not thinking about him—only about myself and my bid to win the Open for the second time in four years. He was through the green in four and I was on in two, and although we had been level when he set off down the par 5 penultimate hole, things looked really rosy for me.

What happened is I suppose a piece of dramatic history of a marvellous championship—a slice of Open action that was inspirational as far as he was concerned, though soul destroying for me. He chipped in and I three-putted. He made 5 and I took 6, giving him the edge going up the last. What happened there that Saturday afternoon—a marvellous hot summer afternoon in Scotland—affected me enough to influence the whole of the rest of my career. I was never again a major force in an Open championship. Lee Trevino that afternoon broke my heart. I'm convinced that chipping in from the rough behind the green was one of those golfing moments he could never have repeated had he tried the shot 500 times, like that chip-in Tom Watson produced at the seventeenth at Pebble Beach to beat Jack Nicklaus in the US Open in 1982.

I've watched film of what happened again and again and I wince every time I see it. He was so casual, so nonchalant, and I agree with his caddy Willie Aitchison that he really had mentally decided that victory was not going to be his . . . but then he produced a shot in a million at just the time it mattered. End of story. He was incredibly casual, certainly looking as if he had mentally conceded, but of course he had been in tremendous form around the greens all week. Four times he holed from off the green and he finished the third round with six straight birdies. When the ball disappeared like a rabbit scuttling into its burrow I was, to say the least, staggered, but I was professional enough not to let it throw me. After all I still had a birdie putt and I was thinking about that. Even if I missed I knew that two putts still left us tied on the leader board with one to play. I still felt in a reasonably strong position. My immediate reaction was that what he had done was incredible but I was still going to win.

Unfortunately I took a rush at the putt—sent it 4ft past and missed the short one. I did not three-putt because I was nervous—I three-putted because I was too aggressive. With the adrenalin flowing I was just too aggressive. I thought, Lee you son-of-a-bitch I'll make this putt for 4 and show you. It was not a bad putt. I could have rolled it close, not gone for it, I suppose, but you don't win championships by playing safe and I was confident enough in my own mind to believe that I would get the birdie anyway. When I three-putted I knew I had lost. I did not even finish second because the charging Jack Nicklaus, shooting 66 on the final day, slipped into runner-up spot after Lee parred the last and I, the heart ripped out of me, dropped another shot.

When we both walked off the seventeenth I raced to the tee, eager to get on down the last, eager to make the birdie to tie him again, though I had a fatalistic attitude and sensed it was not going to be my week. Lee ambled to the tee, keeping me waiting, giving me more time to think about what had just happened. He knew he had the edge then and took full advantage psychologically. I am sure I would have done the same, it's all part of the game. At the end he had no apology to make for what he had done. He was too ecstatic at what had happened. The circumstances had contrived to make me the loser and him the winner for the second year running. I stepped off that eighteenth a shattered man, broken by what had happened.

Twenty minutes earlier I had been on top of the world, not over-confident, not at all arrogantly expecting to win but quietly within myself doing everything to make victory possible. From being poised to enjoy what would have been an even greater moment in my golfing life—winning a second time—I had been drained, cruelly stripped of my moment of glory. What I had had going for me at this time more than anything else was a tremendous confidence, a tremendous belief in myself as a golfer, a competitor, a winner, but that Saturday afternoon everything had disintegrated before my eyes. Trevino had not only chipped in but he had done it at the most crucial time he could. If it had happened on the first hole I could have coped, would have had time to recover, no doubt would have laughed and smiled across at him. Then it would not have been such a knock-out blow mentally as well as in reality. There was nothing I could do to console myself as Vivien and I stood behind the eighteenth green I had played probably better in that Open than in any Open—certainly better than I had when I won at Lytham—but I had lost. I felt the way Tom Weiskopf must have felt three years later when after giving his all at the US Masters at Augusta—a title he had dreamed of winning and kept coming desperately close to grasping— he watched as Jack Nicklaus pipped him and Johnny Miller on the last. At a press conference after the Green Jacket ceremony Tom was in the press tent and told pressmen honestly, emotionally, sadly, that there was nothing he could say. He had given his all and played his heart out and lost. He was numb—as numb as I was in 1972.

I went into total shock for 24 hours, took at least a week to recover something like my old poise and never again recaptured the old magic. No single act by any other golfer so affected my career as that chip-in by Lee Trevino. I felt even worse than Arnold Palmer did at the Olympic Club, San Francisco in 1966 when, heading for victory in the US Open and leading by seven shots with nine to play, he was caught and eventually lost a play-off. It takes a while to recover from that kind of sledgehammer blow and I never really did. I soldiered on, of course, but I was honestly never the same again. Looking back, the rest of that day is a blank, as if my mind had decided to erase it, get rid of the bad memories. I cannot remember what we ate that night, and I am not exactly sure with whom we dined at Greywalls, that lovely hotel alongside the clubhouse of the Honourable Company of Edinburgh golfers. No doubt I was so dazed at what had happened that I acted like a mildly punch-drunk heavyweight. I had to keep reminding myself of the detail of the last two holes—the incredible facts that had conspired to rob me of victory. He had been unbelievably lucky but, looking back, maybe he deserved to win, luck or no luck.

Lee is an extremely tough competitor who has himself coped with tremendous problems throughout his career. His drive, his resilience in adversity, is legendary. I had and still have a great working relationship with him. I am looking forward to being opposing captain to him in the Ryder Cup at The Belfry. We have never been close friends, but that's the case with most of us on tour. If you are playing against fellows every week you don't make too many close relationships. Competitiveness comes in the way of lasting, deep friendships. If you get too close it could become embarrassing for both players. The incredible thing is that there is so little aggravation or unpleasantness on tour. I can think of very few cases of golfers upsetting each other on the course, although strangely I can recall being upset by Brian Barnes once so much so that I requested not to be paired with him for a while. It was at Porthcawl in the Welsh Classic that the incident happened. I hit my ball on to the last green and got a reasonable round of applause. Brian then played almost as close to the stick but did not produce the response from the crowd that I had drawn. As he walked on to the green he turned and in that larger-than-life manner of his asked the spectators why they had not clapped as loud for him. He went on to hole his putt and I missed, and as I walked off I asked him if that made him any happier. Maybe I was extra tense that day but I felt his behaviour was less than professional.

Barnes does get away with a lot—or used to. He does not play so much main tournament golf any more. He is into company days and I know he does them exceptionally well. He cares far more about his golf and his performances than some people ever believed. He could lull the fans into thinking he didn't care but he always did, very deeply. His attitude was his way of coping with pressure. I am sure there are no hard feelings any more, but that day in Wales I was mad at the big fellow whose golfing talent was so great but who just lacked the stomach to win a really big title. It would have been great if he could have won an Open and matched the feat of his father-in-law, Max Faulkner, but it was not to be.

What might have happened to me and my career had I won in 1972? Not a great deal I think—because the family ties would always have been stronger than the urge to keep slogging away on the US Tour. I think when you have done something, that's it. You've given it a good shot and I'd won the Open. I feel just the same way about tournament play—I've done it, given myself a crack at it, but it's time to move on to other things. I've said many times it takes more guts to quit than to carry on sometimes, and I don't think I lack guts.

It would have been the easiest thing in the world for me just to keep on playing like everybody else seems to do and just become another name on another draw sheet—a name with a history behind it but now just making up the numbers—but my heart is not in it any more. The problem is that tournament golf is so demanding that there is no time to get involved in anything else. The commitment to tour play is total. When you are not actually doing it you are thinking about it. It envelops you like an unseen cloud. I'm happy I don't have to go out any more and grind away in tournaments. I have not got to look forward to five or even more years battling on, trying to make a reasonable living and haunted by a great past, by performances I can no longer produce or be expected to produce.

9
Misery on the Greens

By 1973 I was beginning to have problems with my game. The main thing that worried me, that kept me awake at night, was my putting. That was the killer. The long game never bothered me one bit. Hitting the ball was never a problem until I stepped on to the green, and then my knees turned to jelly and my hands felt like two pieces of lead at the end of my arms. I have always been very sensitive to atmosphere. I felt that after I had won the British and US Open titles that the public, the press, everybody, expected me to win with ease the lesser tournaments on the British circuit. They just had to be a breeze for me—if I had won the Open surely it was easy to win the Benson & Hedges, the Carrolls Irish Open (I missed that for a number of years because of the IRA troubles—I was threatened once, and once is enough), the Old Martini and the like. I suppose you could not blame people for thinking that way but the problem was that when I did not win everyone started asking what had gone wrong.

So I started to push even harder for myself, because my pride was being seriously dented, and for the public who had come to expect performances above the ordinary from me. I did not want to let them down. I kept saying to myself that I was too much of a perfectionist, that the putting lapses were only temporary. So I kept at it—stupidly on reflection. I was pushing myself so hard that, far from my putting problems improving, they began to get worse. I got to the point where I was really afraid of going out on to the course because I had forgotten how to putt . . . yet I had been paid appearance money and I was expected to provide the crowds with something to cheer. It eventually got so bad that the sponsors paying the appearance money instituted a clause in my contracts saying that they would not pay out in full unless I made the halfway cut. It was awful but I could see their reasoning. If I was not producing then I should not get the top payment. At the time I probably did not see their point of view as clearly as I do now. People in those days who watched me shoot high scores (by my standards), and then saw me fretting on the greens, no doubt thought I was crazy to have let just one aspect of the game—albeit a vitally important one—get to me, especially since I had clearly putted well to win the two big ones at Lytham and Hazeltine, but they did not appreciate what pressure can do to a man, how it can make him only a fraction of the player he has been.

In the mid and late '70s, when I was in the heat of the battle being watched by hundreds, sometimes thousands, of golf fans waiting for the birdies and I could not produce, it was depressing—and I could not vent my annoyance because golf is not that kind of game. Instead of blowing up I tried harder to get things right and the harder I tried the worse my situation became. Pressure eats away at a man's confidence and, with the benefit of hindsight, I would say that I did not handle the complaint properly. I tried to play the problem out of my system, refusing to give up, when I should have adopted a much less tense attitude and—more importantly—taken time off, and to hell with the appearance money. Maybe I should have adopted a more laid-back approach, like the one Brian Barnes or sometimes Lee Trevino adopt when things are not going right. They shrug their shoulders, smile and decide to come back tomorrow, next week, the following month, and hope it will be better. Unfortunately I could never do that. It just was not my style. I could never get to the point where what I was doing did not matter because it did matter. It mattered very deeply to me. As I said earlier I had always believed that any rewards you get in life are in direct ratio to what you put into it, and in my case I wanted desperately to give value for money in order to maintain the Jacklin image. Regrettably sometimes I failed. Sometimes I did not live up to the expectations everyone else had of me.

I say in all modesty that throughout my career I was a crowd-puller. I created a tremendous atmosphere, and when I was firing on all cylinders I had a huge gallery cheering me on—and I loved the cheers, was inspired by them. If I thrilled people with my golf then you could bet ninety times out of a hundred that the golf I played was thrilling me. I loved it when it was flowing, when the birdies went down on the card as regularly as clockwork, but when the pressure started to prevent that happening I hated it, really hated it. I was in such a state that I could stand over a putt and not remember hitting it, literally could not remember the club hitting the putter face. I used to stand as if in a daze, as if in a dream world, only it was a nightmare world for me. Everything I thought began to be negative. That made the tension worse. I forced myself into thinking only about not missing the putt rather than holeing it, to try to solve my dilemma, but that was even more negative. The putter did not flow. The whole essence of good putting is that the feeling in your hands is transferred to the club head and the flow helps you get the ball in the hole. That feeling is an essential part of the game . . . and I had lost it. I was obstructing the flow.

Putting is a unique combination of the mental and physical processes in golf. The mind tells the hands what to do and they do it naturally. My hands would not work because my mind was passing the wrong signal. I did not realise why but it was because I was mentally exhausted. I remember I played one tournament at Sandwich in which I lined the putter up square with the hole on my intended line then tried looking away as I putted, but the ball still did not go in. That was not the answer. After lining up at another event I turned my head away as I hit the ball . . . and missed far more often than I holed—hardly surprising on reflection. I even closed my eyes and tried to putt from memory, conjuring up in my mind's eye great putts that I had holed on the way to some of my more notable victories, and the ball still edged past, spun out, stopped short but did not go in. I ruined putters trying to bend the heads this way and that. I tried to putt with only my left hand on the shaft, with only my right hand on it, with hands separated, with the left below the right (the way Bernhard Langer of West Germany holes short putts). I closed my stance,

94

widened it, but to no avail. I used thin golf-club grips, thick grips, even no grip at one point.

Nothing I tried made the putting any easier—I was looking for the solution everywhere but in the right place. The answer was in my mind, the solution was to back off, but for the life of me I could not see it. The McCormack Organisation continued to firm up deal after deal for me around the world. I flew about, hoping a change of continent, a change of air, might help but of course it never did. I had commitments with clothing companies and club contracts to honour and I just kept going. With hindsight, I should have taken a year off. Vivien suggested that but I paid no heed and anyway it might not have solved the problem. It would have created even more publicity, and when I returned to the tournament scene—refreshed and mentally sharp—there would have been the inevitable question . . . had I got the old magic back? I was cornered. My confidence was shattered. I did not become edgy, testy, act in an unnatural way off the course, because I always had the stable home life, thank God, that Vivien and the family provided. All I know is that for a number of years all I got from the game that had so fascinated me as a youngster, which I genuinely loved, were mental scars. Every day brought me more mental pain. Physical pain is another thing, and I know there are hundreds of people who suffer physical agonies throughout their lives far greater than I have ever experienced, but my torment was mental.

I got to the point where I loathed having to go out because I knew I would face up yet again to disappointment. It was like volunteering to be tortured every day. So I started to play less and it hurt less. The mental anguish did not go away, and the putting never came back completely, but it became livable with . . . just. I suppose I had really gone too far to expect ever to be completely cured. The scars and memories stick, even if you try to think positively and put them out of your mind. I still remember playing in the Madrid Open one year when I was really up-tight. I was acting as if the Madrid Open was one of the most important in the world, which even the nice people in Spain would be last to claim—but it was vitally important to me. I had a foot putt on the last hole—a long par-5 up a hill towards the clubhouse, which stands on the top of the ridge overlooking one of the great cities of Europe. I holed the putt . . . but hit it twice, I was so nervous. I could go on to that same putting green now and try to hit the ball twice as it rolled the 2in before it dropped and I would find it very, very difficult to do. It was just that my body was not in tune with my brain. They were operating separately because my brain, my subconscious, was trying to tell me I needed a break and I could not decode the message.

What made it worse was that I had no one I could turn to for help, because nobody understood my problem. The well-known golfing teachers could not help me because the problem I had was not a technical one. John Jacobs, who knows everything about technique, could hardly have been expected to know anything about the kind of pressure I was experiencing. He could not know what I was suffering because he had never suffered it himself. Henry Cotton, winner of three Open championships, is a lovely man, a great man, but I knew he did not appreciate what I was going through when he talked to me about knowing it was time for him to give up top-line golf when he could not hit the par-5 greens in two. For all his experience he had never encountered the pressure the modern tournament pro can find himself having to cope with. Today we play a minimum of 30 tournaments a year, while Henry at the top was playing half that number if he was lucky. It is ironic really. He probably wished there had been twice as many tournaments for him to play in his day, whereas I was wanting to play only half the number I did.

During my bad spell when the putting really was getting me down I used to take sleeping tablets—just to make sure I could get off to sleep and not lie awake worrying. The problem was that I could not work out why my putting was so poor. I took so long to realise that basically I just was not enjoying playing tournament golf any more, that I was flogging a dead horse. I was very unhappy. I was miserable on the course and more than anything else the one thing I did not want to do was go into a tournament and be drawn with younger players. I was not worried about the fact that they might score lower than I could, although I'd be trying like the devil—I just did not want the younger fellows to get to the stage where they did not want to play with me because I was a miserable old bastard—which in fairness I often was. The last thing I wanted was for them to be saying, when they saw they were paired with me, 'What will he be moaning about today?' Because I did moan. All I wanted to do, if I was putting badly and missing short putts I formerly holed without thinking, was to do it quietly and disappear without saying anything to anyone. Ultimately, as the problem stays with you month after month, you can become consumed by it. I did and I felt it was better to back out quietly, just step away from it, which is really what I did eventually. There is plenty more life to live, and it is not all about holeing putts.

I've seen what bitterness can do to players. I've seen fellows who are not naturally miserable become that way because they are devoted to shooting low scores and cannot for one reason or another do so. It is bound to gnaw away inside a player, and tragically that inward frustration, anxiety and annoyance not only affect your game—they affect your personality and your appeal to the public, and eventually your reputation suffers. A dear friend of mine, Marshall Bellow, with whom I stay in Leeds every time I go up there once told me, 'I don't want to go and watch Tony Jacklin shooting 73 and 74. Of course you are not wanting to shoot these scores yourself. Of course you are trying damned hard to shoot 68 but in your heyday when you were at the top you were shooting low scores and I'd rather remember you like that. You'd be better off not doing it at all if you cannot regularly break 70'. And he was right in one respect. The problem was that even when I was not shooting the low figures I once did the fans still turned out to watch me. It's just the same with Arnold Palmer in the States. It is 20 years since he won a major, ten since he won a tournament, yet you can be sure he has one of the largest galleries every week he plays because he still has the charisma. He is remarkable. His enthusiasm for the game has lasted much longer than mine. He still loves it, you see. He thrives on the roar of the crowd and will never

97

give up until he really is forced to. Jack Nicklaus will, I fancy, ease himself out quickly when he decides he has had enough. He will not hang on Palmer-style.

When I was shooting poorish (for me) scores, I still did not think there was a lot wrong with my game—just my putting. I went for years with an average of 30 putts a round. I never ever had a season when I averaged lower than 30 and we all know that winners on tour these days average 28 putts a round. More often than not, and allowing for the few times when my streaky putting came good, I would take 32 putts a round—I'd give a dozen shots to the field over the week and still managed sometimes to win. I tried so hard to make my putting more consistent. I practised and practised. I read and reread books on positive thinking. I tried all kinds of putters—upright ones, blades, centre-shafted ones, putters with mallet heads—and nothing worked, because the problem was in my mind. Putting when it worked well for me was pure and instinctive. There was the ball, there was the hole, this was the line—the putter was in your hand, you hit the ball and, bang! You not only expected the ball to disappear down the hole, it did. Then as you push yourself along you become mentally tired, and physically exhausted—a lethal combination. All of a sudden your confidence is totally eroded, it all becomes so much of an effort. Children don't find putting a bore. You don't get a fourteen-year-old going on to a practice putting green and yipping putts. Why not? Because they are fresh and eager and not the victims of the horrible pressure the Royal and Ancient game puts you under. I was a victim.

At the Uniroyal at Moor Park in 1977 (Severiano Ballesteros beat Nick Faldo in a play-off), nobody knew that I spent a little time each day before I played with a Harley Street specialist. My old friend Johnny Rubens from Potters Bar days knew him and thought he might be able to relax me enough to enable me to get everything back into perspective and more importantly to get my putting back on song. He had used the fellow to help him relax after a period of severe hypertension. I gave him a chance. I told him that I was so tense about my putting that when I walked on to a green I was totally embarrassed. I really found it difficult to speak about it. I was in a state of total fear because of the importance I had put on this aspect of the game. I went to him every day for a half an hour and he tried to hypnotise me and he just couldn't—I was too strong willed a person. He would sit me down and ask me what I enjoyed doing most, what made me really happy. I would suggest I found cutting the grass very therapeutic. Quietly he would talk me through the whole operation: setting out the mower, emptying the box of cuttings, doing the borders and, after it is all over, on a hot summer's afternoon, slipping into the kitchen for a cool beer from the fridge. Then a seat on the patio and a glance at how good the lawn looks–a feeling of total satisfaction! Hard though he tried, however, I could not help but see holes in that lawn and imaginary flags sticking out of them, and I could not erase the thought of having to hole putts on that beautiful lawn and missing and being terribly disheartened. Maybe the enjoyable activity I chose was wrong, and I should have stayed away from grass altogether. I knew what he was trying to do and I knew he had no chance of doing it with me. It really was a wasted effort, but I was willing to try anything to find the solution to the problem. He never really got my mind off golf.

I was anxious about the putting but I was frustrated, too, about not winning any more, because I knew I was capable of winning. I was, after all, a better player than everyone else, but instead of winning half a dozen times a year I won a couple. One year it was ridiculous. I was almost never out of the top four and should have won eight tournaments—I was certainly in a position to do so—and won once. It was desperate. Yet I could not talk it out with anyone on tour because everyone was a competitor and an opponent far more interested in his own problems than mine. I am not saying that no one is helpful on tour—they are—but there is a vast difference between chatting on the surface about the problem, as I did with a lot of people, and sitting down and analysing the situation deeply. I never spoke in depth to a single soul about my problem.

What was so galling was that, during the 1971 Open, John Jacobs came to help me sort out a long-game technical snag that had cropped up. He did his best to put me right but it is tough during a championship as big as the Open to make any technique changes, however minor, and I soldiered on—putting like a magician—to finish third. That was the rub—I remembered so well how effectively I could putt on occasions and that made my problem seem even more acute. The snag was that apart from the putting I was still playing reasonably well. I never went completely off, never got bad enough to realise I needed a complete rest. I never even considered that I was not winning as often as I should because I was playing too much. How easy it is now to see what the solution was. I may not have psychologically, mentally, wanted to play but financially I was being driven on. I had the family to support and there were the responsibilities we had for Viv's folks and my own. I was employing staff. I was directly or indirectly responsible for nine or ten people, so I maintained my stupid, punishing, mentally crippling schedule.

I always prided myself on my independence—the ability at any time to turn round and say no, if I didn't feel like doing something. I had worked hard to get into the position of being financially well off enough to be independent like that. Yet I hardly ever took advantage of the position I had worked for. I hardly ever said no.

It is circumstances that make putting difficult. God knows how many letters I have had from interested fans over a long time offering help. Yet in certain weeks in my career there has been no better putter in the world. All the people who very kindly wrote to me suggesting I try this method or that were really quite naïve to think that I would not have tried everything having played the game for almost 30 years, but it was nice they should try to help. I once asked Deane Beman, who now runs the US Tour, what the single most important thing was about putting and he said it was to believe that you were going to hole it–a positive state of mind. If you had that, you probably could hole out with anything because it had nothing to do with your method or the equipment being used. Peter Alliss once asked the great Byron Nelson the same question and he said that he did not know what he did or why he putted well! I suspect it was instinct—lose that and you have a problem, a problem that will not go away—or will hardly ever go away.

Much as I admired Henry Longhurst and that famous column of his in the *Sunday Times*, contrary to what he said it *is* possible to get rid of the yips. Bernhard Langer got rid of them, or has for the moment. God forbid that they should ever come back to haunt him, but I suspect he will have to work extremely hard to avoid having a recurring problem. Maybe when the enthusiasm has waned a bit, when he no longer relishes the pressure-packed lifestyle, they will reappear, but for the moment he has conquered them and that's great. It shows what great willpower he has—the mental strength that will win more major championships. He deserves all the glory he can find. I have more respect for him and what he has done to solve his problem than anyone I have known in golf. His is an incredible recovery. I know what he suffered because I have putted so badly at times that I have experienced the horror. I've stood on the green in a tournament facing up to a ten-footer and found myself shivering. I was so out of touch I was just as likely to hit the ball off the green!

Every ounce of feeling had left my hands and my brain was numb. Yet when I have putted well I've almost seen the ball linger on the putter head and stay there for a split second before heading unerringly for the hole. The feeling you have is so perfect that as you stand over the ball you really do not want to hit it—you want to spin out the pleasure of the sensation as long as possible. Too often, however, when I was delaying my putting it was not because I was savouring the moment, rather I was loathing it and was not able to work out how best to hit it! I hit so many good putts that did not go in over the years, that brushed the hole and stayed out, that I became almost neurotic. Yet I cannot say that it was putting that cost me other major wins because it was not. In the majors, curiously, I never putted all that badly.

Being happy in life, being happy in what you are doing, is what it is all about, and there are so many more important things than golf for me now—my health, my family's health—and when you get to 41 and have made your way in the world you can relocate golf well down the list of priorities. Yet for long enough putting was an obsession, a No. 1 priority, because if I could not putt well my earning capacity would be badly hit.

10
Problems Unanswered

My routine never changed during the period when I had all my putting problems. I tried to carry on as normally as possible, of course, but what used to frustrate me was the total lack of understanding of the situation from people whom I appreciate were only trying to help. They would talk to me about how differently I was swinging to the way I swung the club when I won at Lytham. Even senior professionals on tour seemed to have no idea where the real problem lay for me—in my head. But then no one had experienced what I was experiencing. How on earth do you simulate pressure in a practice-round? You cannot. You cannot put someone on the eighteenth and say, 'Here's a £2,000 putt. I bet you cannot hole it from 2ft'. Pressure is a build-up over months and years of holeing putts to win and missing putts. All have an effect on what you think when you get over a vital putt in a championship, like the putt Doug Sanders faced to win the Open in 1970 at St Andrews. He has been criticised for missing it. The putt has been described as all sorts of distances but it was a very missable putt and one of the most difficult you can get—slightly downhill, breaking left to right. Two and a half feet to test nerve and concentration. Two and a half killing feet to win the greatest championship of all. Circumstances meant that it was his one chance to win and he missed, but it is the easiest thing in the world to criticise the golfers if you are watching on television in the warmth of your own sitting-room. Sanders was a professional doing his best. He had come halfway round the world to try to win the championship. His was not an awful putt, as I have heard some people say—it was a sad one, coming as it did when it did.

A professional has to block out the day-to-day problems

103

of life—the kind of things we all face up to. If somebody was really ill at home then I would just withdraw, but if I had a tiff with Viv (and we don't often have tiffs) I would find it easy to block it out! I may be luckier than most in that respect. I might feel a little concerned, but I could forget about it completely as I played round. My concentration would be that complete—or would have been when I was at the top. Later on I would have found it more difficult, I'm sure, as I began to struggle with my putting. Mark James suffers a bit from the problems of an ill-disciplined putter, but I think he is his own enemy in that he appears to react so despairingly. He gets so down in the dumps. You cannot afford to feel like that. I kept trying to lick it, and worked hard to cure it—as I am sure he is doing, but he does look so depressed sometimes that I cannot help but think he is sometimes letting it beat him.

For someone like me, who has been such an indifferent putter on average through the years, it is remarkable that there have been weeks when I have been walking on air, when the hole has looked as big as a bucket. I shot 27 under par in Colombia once—that's the best golf I've ever played. I just felt I could do anything that week. Nobody could have beaten me. I ate well and never had the feeling that the magic would disappear overnight. The next day it would be there again. I wish I knew why but there was no logical reason. I think I was caught up with the idea that the longer I played the more chance I had of sorting my putting out—it's an extension of the thought that the more you play the more your chance of winning improves, but I know now that's poppycock. Some players wait a heck of a long time for a win—for some their great day never ever comes.

Golf has always been an easy game for me. If I did not play now for a year I know that within two weeks I could be competing again reasonably well—at least I would be hitting the ball solidly enough. I know what makes my swing work; I am totally happy about the mechanics. I worked hard when I was younger to perfect that swing, because I knew I needed a good foundation. I know fellows with poor swings who practise so hard—but then they have to because if they did not their game would disintegrate. If they would only consider making a few changes to improve their basic method they might not need to practise so much. Once you are doing it right, the technique is there forever. It's just like walking. Once you learn to walk, you are not constantly falling in the street. You don't totter about for more than the first few weeks and then before you know where you are you can run as well. Some golfers on tour listen to so many theories about their swings that they get confused and never get it right. I would need two honours degrees from Oxford to understand what some of them are talking about when they discuss technique. It should all be kept simple.

One fellow who helped me a lot—I understand his thinking—was Bob Toski. What a great teacher! He gave me one of the best putting tips I ever had (mind you most of them are the best for as long as the putts drop!) He watched me putt at a tournament in Florida where I had indicated I was in trouble. He told me I was a great putter and that the only problem was I was not letting it happen. I let it happen and finished third that week at Doral. Maybe it would have helped me had I had a guru standing by all the time! He might have been able to see quicker than me what was wrong with my mental approach and why.

What happened to me is there to see in others. We put the putting problems that plagued Ben Hogan and Sam Snead in their later years down to other things, but if I had been really clever I would have looked more closely at what was happening to them and why. They had pushed too far and the mind was telling them to quit in the only way it knew how. It didn't happen to Billy Casper, Jerry Barber or Bobby Locke, but then they were all golfers who with the best will in the world were not all that good through the green. I know Locke won four Opens but he was a magician with the putter because he had to be. It's strange but the fellows whose long game is very good end up with putting problems, and the golfers whose long game is not top class never have any serious problems on the greens. Nicklaus is the exception to this rule but then he is exceptional in every sense, which is why he has won twice as many majors as anyone else, why at 45 he is still as much of a threat when he tees up as he was 25 years ago. The guys who had cracked the game tee to green—Snead, Nelson, Hogan—all ended up with putting problems because the human body will do so much and no more.

An indifferent long-game player will reach the green and know he has to make the putt to maintain his score. You might think the pressure on him is greater than the pressure on the golfer on the same green going for a birdie but it is not. You always have in your mind a score you know you have to shoot to be up among the leaders. Take Wentworth, for instance, when we are playing a stroke-play competition round the Burma Road, the famous west links. I would know that if I shot 67 or 68 I'd be in reasonable shape, 69 or 70 is OK; you know that you will be with two dozen others if you shoot par; and higher than that is no good. Whatever we end up scoring I know when we start out what the number for me is that day, and if it is 67 and I get to the turn in 32 the pressure is on—the pressure to lead and eventually to win. Take, on the other hand, someone like Deane Beman or Jerry Barber who relied heavily on their putting ability. They would be powder-puff hitters through the green and always expecting to shoot in the low 70s. If their putting was off it was mid 70s. They seldom had to face up to the pressures of winning because as often as not they were never in a position to, and they never had any real putting problems because that was the strength of their games. It had to be. I would be being far too boastful if I put myself into the Hogan or Snead class, but in my case the better a player I became and the closer to the pin I hit the ball, the lower my potential scoring ability was. I knew that a 66 or 67 would be easy if I putted at all well. All the time you are thinking about putting because the rest of the game is easy. Then when you set off you hit every green in par and none of the birdie putts drop and you are totally frustrated. If, on the other hand, you miss the first five greens and have to get up and down for par you find a way to save the day, you find a way to coax them into the hole. If I had a bad day and missed greens it was incredible how I used to get up and down from traps, how I would chip dead or roll a long one in to stop dropping a shot but, faced with the same putt for birdie, I would miss them half the time. Mind you, when you play like a 'charlie' and you still shoot par you get a great kick out of your escape act! In a way it was fun but I would know that I did not want to play that way again the next day because playing like that does not win tournaments.

What I think I am trying to say is that the less capable player, that is the golfer who has not got the gift of striking the ball consistently well all the time, struggles from tee to green but usually putts well.

Why should putting be tougher for the pro going for the low score? Let's take as an example Gary Player and Jack Nicklaus playing an imaginary round in the World Match Play. Nine times out of ten Gary would beat Jack. Gary would wear him down with shots that Nicklaus really could not quite understand. Jack would hit every green in par with great high shots from the middle of the fairway. Gary, in the rough off the tee, would more than likely zigzag his way to a birdie to win or at worst half a hole. Nicklaus would have played it much better and have gained little or no advantage. As they walk from green to tee who is in the best frame of mind? Player is buoyant; Nicklaus is perplexed. Player wins.

When I was in a trauma about my putting I asked Bobby Locke for his help and advice, but all he said was that he 'put drop spin on the ball, Master'. He meant he just holed everything as if by second nature. He had no conception of the mental pressure I was going through. Nor, for that matter, did Hogan have much idea about the psychological side of golf. He was a golfing mechanic. I never spoke to Hogan about my putting problem because I knew he (1) would not be interested and (2) would not know the answer. I never asked Jack Nicklaus either. I suppose when the putting problems really started I had stopped playing regularly in America. I could have phoned him—but I'll tell you why I did not. It was as a result of a conversation I had with him at one of the Ryder Cups. I was sitting with Tommy Horton and Brian Barnes and we were discussing whether golf was a left- or right-sided game. I said that I believed it to be a left-sided game. They both disagreed so I

107

called in Jack, whom I knew agreed with my view, if his books were anything to go by anyway. Any book he had ever had written for him said that he felt it was left-sided. Yet that night he said he thought it was right-sided. You could have floored me with a feather duster. I don't know whether he was trying to be funny on that occasion or bloodyminded or what, but he can be like that. He is the sort of chap who would ask your opinion on something then immediately totally disagree with your view as if trying to create an argument. I don't know why he does it. He's been at the top for twenty years and doesn't need to behave like that. It's just his way. I knew there was no point in trying to get him to help me with my problem.

There is a limit for every sportsman beyond which he dare not go. There is a line he must not cross, at the risk of losing his form, his reputation and everything he has worked so hard to achieve. The body and the brain know the limit, and if you go beyond it, they react to make what you normally enjoy doing a real effort and strain. It is at this point that the sensible sportsman or woman slows down. I crossed the line and for two or so years did myself no good, even if I did keep collecting appearance money from sponsors. Maybe Max Faulkner had it right (although I did not think so at the time) when I talked to the last man to win the Open for Britain before I took the title in 1969. Explaining my anxiety about putting he told me, in his own inimitable way, 'Tony, you are like me—face up to the fact that you cannot do it any more'. I laughed and thought he was crackers but if he meant I had burned myself out by playing too often, by trying too hard, he was probably right.

There was not even another top sportsman in another field who could help, and goodness knows plenty of the stars were signed up by the same organisation that handled me—the Mark McCormack Group. In fact the only golfer who did help me, later—much later—on, was Ben Crenshaw, who won the US Masters in 1984 to become one of the most popular winners of all time. He had been so often the bridesmaid that it looked as if he was never going to win a big one, but he did, bringing more than a tear or two to a few eyes. He is one of the most popular guys in golf and what he said made more sense to me than anything else I had been told regarding a cure for the putting yips. We were playing in a tournament in the States and he came up to me, commenting that he had been watching me for some time and knew I had had putting troubles for years. I had, and although it really became bad in the years following my major wins, I'd had indications in the late '60s that when I was mentally or physically not at my best it would be my putting that would suffer. In fact I can even remember the first time I hit a putt and suffered that sinking feeling in my stomach. It was at Palm Springs on one of the back nine greens on the Indian Wells Club built in the lee of a huge escarpment. I had a putt from 20ft and I rolled it towards the hole but my hands did not do what they were supposed to do. The ball went close to the hole all right but I knew something was wrong. I could not figure out what.

Up until that point in my career every putt I ever hit was a mind-to-hand thing, totally natural, but that incident at Indian Wells heralded what was to happen later in my career. If only I had taken more time to analyse what had gone wrong, I could have prevented all the suffering of the mid '70s, but I was not that clever—and anyway I was so busy playing I almost did not have time to think. The incident at Indian Wells happened just as I began pushing myself relentlessly to the top. The problem is that you do not lose your putting touch overnight. It is a gradual thing. You putt well enough most of the time to blot out the poor putting rounds, but then the ratio gradually changes. At first you might not even believe it because any golfer worth his salt is trained to think positively, but that positive approach can sometimes blot out the reality of the situation. Looking back, I'm only too well aware that putting was the one aspect of the game that always bothered me. Before all the big events I had few doubts about my own ability to win if I putted well. I knew that if the ball started dropping and red figures went on the board that would be a tremendous inspiration. If I putted well I believed that winning for me was then a foregone conclusion. There was nothing I could not achieve if the putter was working. If it was not then winning was impossible. Putting was everything to me—bold aggressive putting which ended with the ball rattling into the cup the way Arnold Palmer used to hole out.

What Crenshaw suggested was a change of attitude. He had been offered this advice early in his career to help him on the greens. He told me that it is psychologically sensible to hit the ball close to the hole and not go for everything. This style of play eased the pressure, reduced the tension and, he said, I would be surprised how many of the putts actually did go in—because I was not expecting them to. He agreed that it might seem daft to have any aim other than getting all putts into the hole first time, but he argued that if you do not expect to hole every putt then the ones that go in are a massive morale-booster. Far better that than going into a downer every time you miss. Ben said he imagined a sort of 6in wide track down which the ball had to roll to the hole, which instantly eliminated working out whether the ball should be right lip, inside right lip, outside right lip, left lip, inside or outside left.

Everything Ben did was based on the assumption that when you start to putt badly it is because you are trying to be far too precise, and worrying too much about the line, and of course he had a point. I remember once asking Bob Charles in a practice round what he thought the line was to the hole and he replied, 'About straight, I think'. I was flabbergasted. Bob has over the years been one of golf's great putters. He was doing naturally what Ben was advocating I should do to try to solve my problems. In my good years I would not have entertained the thought of not going for every putt, but I was desperate so I tried the Crenshaw psychology for a time—and it worked. That is, it worked for a time, but it was terribly difficult for me. Every time I walked on to the green I was reminding myself to relax, and trying to convince myself that it did not matter whether I holed the putt or not. I would take two practice swings and try to keep everything free and easy. The problem was that I felt I was being so negative that all the antics were only reminding me I had the yips—me, Tony Jacklin. It was unthinkable but it was true. True I did not yip every putt I hit but I can tell you that eight out of every ten putts I have hit in tournaments in the last ten years have not

110

been hit in anything like the way I wanted to hit them. It is a staggering admission but it is true. I was happy with only 20 per cent of the putts I hit in ten years.

My experimentation continued as I tried to control the disease. I sometimes took the putter back and hit the ball pendulum-style, following through as far as I had taken the club head from the ball. I was trying to get the ball to roll the way it had for me in the early days but it would not. I was shocked when I saw where some of my putts ended up—because there was no co-ordination. Then one day I was staying with a millionaire friend in Palm Springs and he had on his bookshelf *The Inner Game of Tennis*, a forerunner to Timothy Galwey's book *The Inner Game of Golf*. Both books were concerned with the psychological aspect of the game, of controlling it well enough to be able to produce your best most of the time. I read the tennis book and could see the parallels in golf. It had a real impact on me and I really did work hard, in the days afterwards, at backing off, at not taking the business quite so seriously, but at the end of each round—in the glaring sunshine which did not help—I was drained. I would go back to the house, flop down on the bed and sleep for two hours or even longer. I just went out cold. I was trying to cure a psychological problem by putting even more pressure on my psychological capacities. I was exhausted in body and mind when I reached the eighteenth—and I knew that was unnatural.

I just kept going hoping the problem would mysteriously go away, but problems never do. Tantalisingly, every now and again I would have one of the good old rounds when everything went right and my problems seemed a million miles away. I would earnestly hope the troubles were over but they would be back to plague me again the next day. I still had the monkey on my back—he had just had a day off. When the monkey took a week off I won, but not nearly as often as my talent should have allowed. Had I reduced my schedule as I should have done, how many more tournament titles would I have collected? We shall never know the answer but I reckon as many again as I won. Lee Trevino, who is such a philosopher in his own way, said once that God never gave any one person everything. In my case he gave me my putting problems—or did he? It could be argued I gave the problems to myself by trying to do too much and, having caught the disease, I could not diagnose the trouble and suggest a cure. Now, looking back, I can say with absolute certainty that all my problems stemmed from over-stretching myself until, like any rubber band, I snapped. Had I not had a happy home life I might have ended up turning to drink as a temporary solution—but I don't really think so.

Folks would say, Jacko's different from other golfers. He doesn't get nervous, he makes golf look so easy. But latterly I did get nervous and latterly it was not easy at all. When I was winning I always had a jaunty walk, head held high—just like Seve Ballesteros has when he is doing something spectacular today. Latterly I was trying to maintain that confident image but it was all a charade, a painful charade. I didn't lose weight, or show any other outward signs of the conflict going on inside me, but I wanted to sleep all the time. I wished sometimes I could sleep for a week just to be out of it, so I did not have to step on to any greens. All the time I was missing the point, either because I genuinely could not assess the situation or because subconsciously I knew it would cost me a great deal of money if I stopped playing, even temporarily. I suppose deep down I was aware that a golfer's active tournament playing life is necessarily a short one. Deep down I was wrestling with my inner self. I was blind to my natural instinct to slow down in the way I had slowed down as a child. I stayed on the lucrative treadmill, encouraged in this direction by John Jacobs and the PGA European Tour officials, who knew I was a major drawing power in the early days of the circuit that today has grown to over £4 million in prize money. I never doubted I should help. I wanted to. I needed no persuasion—all I needed and never got was a holiday from golf. That was my fault, no one else's.

As I ploughed on I found more and more that my concentration was being affected very badly. I became supersensitive to the clicking of a camera and I have had to put up with more of that than anyone else, with the exception today of Seve and I'm sure Nick Faldo, Bernhard

Langer, Sam Torrance and Sandy Lyle will experience it much more as they continue to enjoy greater and greater success. In the early '70s I was if not the only target certainly the main one. I used to come in and stupidly complain about the camera problem to Neil Coles, chairman of the Tour. He said he did not know what I was talking about, and I know why—it was not often anyone with a camera ever followed him round.

Professional sporting cameramen are never any trouble. There are regular fellows on the Tour who take amazing pictures quietly and efficiently without ever putting any of us off. They are brilliant at their craft, given how touchy we can be, but sometimes some of the papers send along photographers who do not know anything about golf and more importantly do not want to know anyway. They are the rogues who cause the trouble, moving about on the back swing, positioning themselves in the direct line of a putt. They would argue that they are only trying to get the best pictures for their papers, and of course they are, but I wish they would take a few tips from the regulars. Golf is not the kind of sport that lends itself to insensitive cameramen, and it is very special assignment for someone who has a feel for the game. I know how difficult their job is and usually appreciate the problems with which they have to contend, but even the regulars must have been a little jumpy when they were out with me in the mid '70s. I was so edgy I could have heard an eyelid flutter never mind a camera shutter click. Indeed I got to the stage where, I am sure, I began hearing them or put myself off by anticipating a click when none had happened or was going to happen—and all because I could not solve my putting problem.

As an amateur I had never been pressured into playing tournaments. It was only after the big wins that the offers started rolling in from the McCormack Organisation. It was only then I started to overdo it. I got to the stage where if the money was right I'd go anywhere—to Japan, where I still have contracts, or even Australia, where I did not like the way they treated visitors. I thought the Australian attitude to visiting golfers from England was crude to say the least. I hated it when I was called a 'pommy bastard',

113

even if it was said in jest—but I went and I won and the money was good. Now all that unhappiness is behind me. Now golf can begin taking a back seat in the playing sense. I'll play the odd event here and there, of course, but only when I want to, just like I did as a youngster. We've gone full circle. I don't expect so much of myself any more. If I do well and put four steady rounds together in, say, the Open, then that will give me far more satisfaction than having to give a whole year to striving for a win. People may still expect me to be playing the way I did when I won at Lytham but of course I cannot. I can still play well but it's a different Tony Jacklin now.

I've rationalised the situation. I have a responsibility to keep my body and my game in shape. Playing five or six events a year is going to do that without messing me up mentally. I'll always try and do my best, and always hope to do well—I owe that to everyone not least myself—but that Open win was sixteen years ago. My competitive edge is still there, and still hopefully as keen most of the time—but not always. I don't match myself up against other players but with myself in my heyday. I know what to expect and am disappointed if I don't achieve it. I still have standards.

I am not opting out if I do not compare myself with Seve Ballesteros because that would be an unfair comparison. He is moving into his prime; I am past mine and on the point of full retirement. On the day he should always shoot better than me now. He's younger, he's longer, his sharp game is shorter and he is playing more. He has more things going for him than me but just sometimes along the way I might have a better day than him in the same event—that's golf. Seve is a full-time player and I am an ex-player turned businessman—that's the way I see it. I've heard the cheers and enjoyed them but miss them very little. I've had the big time, thank you. I've no incentive to want to play full time again, but if by some miracle something happened which allowed me to walk on to a green without fear again and roll putts casually into the hole like I did in the old days, then I might be tempted to make a comeback. But that's wishful thinking. Miracles don't happen like that, and will not in my case. That's the dreamer in me coming out again—the dreamer who can so easily be suffocated by the realist in my personality. Anyway I'm not looking for a miracle. I've had 20 years of tour golf and have done really quite well. At 41 I'm not going to get any better—I can only get worse. I'm never going to improve on my performances of 1969 and 1970—not now.

I know people will say that I'm maybe opting out too soon, and will point to the fact that Nicklaus, who is five years older, and Player, eight years my senior, are still playing. Nicklaus seems to enjoy it still, but this is only because he has paced himself so well throughout his career, playing 18 or 20 times a year only, hardly ever playing after August. He has never at any stage in his illustrious career attempted to operate my kind of schedule—wise man. He has always rationed his appearances, organising his schedule to be at his best, he hopes, around the majors. He has the ability to take one or two weeks off between tournaments and come back as sharp as he was when he played before. He is lucky, as well as being a golfing genius! I did not manage to opt in and out so effectively. Player has lasted longer than most because he is a record-maker. Gary will keep playing until he drops because he will want to be the oldest this and oldest that. Golf is a drug as far as he is concerned, an occupation which still interests him hugely with the Seniors Tour coming along to offer him the chance of making another million. He may be into horse-racing these days in a big way, at his remarkable new ranch just outside Johannesburg, but he could never give up golf. In that respect he is very like Palmer. It is in their blood, and they compete as if by instinct. They crave for the competition, long for the adulation and enjoy giving thousands of fans considerable pleasure. That's fine for them but I don't envy them one little bit.

I do not need to play on to put something back into the game. I have put plenty back in the past 20 years by playing as well as I did at times, and by giving so much pleasure to people even when I was not enjoying it all that much. I hope that whatever I did and wherever I did it I brought credit to my country, gave value for money. I'm sure I must have let some people down sometimes, or some people may have felt I'd let them down, but I can live with myself on that score. I do not feel that for the rest of life I need to go around doing charitable things for the game and the people in it to try and equalise the amount of money I've made from it. I've earned my good living. I've travelled millions of miles to earn it; I've been away from my family a lot to earn it; I've worked hard for anything I've got and I'm proud of that; I feel no obligation to anyone any more, least of all now that the fun has gone out of playing. The bottom line about my golf is that whatever else I do I'll always be remembered as the British golfer who held golf's two great titles at one time—the Open in 1969, and the US Open in 1970. I won other tournaments including the PGA at Hillside just three years ago, but no one will remember that. Unless I had a real chance of winning another Open I would be wasting my time playing the circuit full time and I would never win another major now. I play golf only if I can get some satisfaction out of it. If I feel I cannot then I simply don't play. To me that makes sense.

11
Split Two Ways

Although ten years of battling with the best took their toll, as inevitably they would, because I did not pace myself properly, I am luckier than most in that I was successful enough in the early part of my career to opt out. Eight out of ten golfers on the European Tour who would love to quit cannot. They need to keep going because they do not have the money behind them to retire, to take up an alternative career. In fact alternatives to playing golf are far from your mind at the start, when everything is going well. I've had the luxury of being able to stop, take time and think about the future, and have had the additional bonus that doors have opened to me that might not have done so but for the fact that I am a former Open champion. The long-term benefits of the Open win have been immense. I may no longer be a top dog competitively but my stock is still high and I believe under my new circumstances I can approach contracts and do deals myself, outside the McCormack framework. McCormack's International Management Group have made a lot of money out of me in the past. They have had good value out of Tony Jacklin, thanks to what they did for me, and I have no guilt feelings about branching out on my own. They have younger stars to turn their attentions to now.

In my day there was no one better than me in Britain and I do believe I knew how good I was. Despite what has happened with prize money in the last five years I can honestly say that I am not envious of anyone. I never have been nor ever will be, and maybe that is because really I have had everything I ever wanted! Unfortunately I have not managed to make quite enough to feel comfortable for the rest of my life but I fancy I shall make a lot of money over the next ten years, more than I've made out of other business I have been involved in, more than I have made out of golf in the past ten! So money really does not bother me. It's the old story—as long as I have got enough to do what I want to, to buy what I want to buy, to live in the manner to which I have become accustomed, I'm happy. I don't regret a minute of my life to date—a life of Rolls-Royces and Mercedes Benz cars, of staff to help around the house. I could never have dreamed I would be that successful all those years ago in Scunthorpe. Or perhaps that's not so—the sky was always my limit.

I've wasted a fortune on cars. I have after all had 35 over the years. Cars—fast cars—have been my only real weakness, which I suppose is better than getting mixed up with fast women and gambling sharks. I have had three Rolls-Royces in my day, a Bentley, an Aston Martin or two, Jensens and Mercedes Benz. The one that gave me most pleasure was my first Rolls—the one I bought after my Open win. It was in 1970 and it cost me £12,200—a brand spanking new Rolls, a two-door Mediterranean blue job with white upholstery, which went like a dream. I kept it for 25,000 miles, then sold it because I thought all Rolls-Royces were perfect. Unfortunately the next one wasn't very good. I did not like it as much and got rid of it very quickly. I wish I had had the sense to keep that first one. It would have been worth a small fortune now. But you know this is life—when you have got what you want, you don't want it any more. As soon as you know it's yours, having fought and worked like hell to get it, it is no longer so important to you. There will always be something else you want. I've been lucky. Anything I've ever really wanted I've been able to afford.

There is nothing now that I would long to have, not even a Lear jet of my own. It would be marvellous to have the jet and the pilot standing by to fly us anywhere at any time but even allowing for the fact that I don't want to travel as much, it would be a ridiculous expense. I started to learn to fly once in Jersey because I thought I might one day have my own plane, but I only did twelve hours. It was going to be far harder work getting the pilot's licence than I anticipated— there was so much homework to do. In addition I happened to have an instructor who fancied himself as an aerobatic ace. We seemed to spend more time flying upside down than the right way up and I think he enjoyed seeing me turning green. Maybe he hated golf. In the end I packed it up.

Considering all the air travel I have done, I have never really cracked jet lag. I've always had problems with it whenever I have gone east-west or vice versa. It's not been so bad going up and down—north–south. I've been affected very badly, not having the ability of Gary Player, the most far-travelled golfer ever, to sleep on planes. He has been known to lie down on the floor between seats just to get a good night's rest!

I never relished the quick trips to America and back because I knew that for the first three days I'd wake up at 4, 5 and then 6 o'clock in the morning, before I got adjusted to US time, and having got adjusted it would be time for me to jump on a plane and fly back to face another tedious readjustment period. It is even worse for me on trips to Japan or Australia. I reckon that Mark McCormack, who keeps such detailed records of his travel that he could tell you to the last mile how far he has travelled since he started in the business, moves about so much that jet lag must never catch him up! He really is an iron man. I cannot take a fraction of what he endures each year by choice. I've tried sleeping pills, but I'm afraid that if I take them and there is an emergency they wouldn't be able to wake me up. Can you imagine the plane being evacuated and everyone saying, 'Oh, just leave him—he's sound asleep . . .' No thank you.

In my early days I dreamed of being a star and I suppose there is a bit of a showman in me. I enjoy responding to the applause and the cheers. I enjoy being recognised, up to a point. It's handy if you want the best table in a restaurant but being recognised has its disadvantages too. I don't like big crowds, which means I have a love-hate relationship with the Open. I love the championship for what it represents. I love it for the history and the tradition and because I am one of the élite group of modern British golfers who have won it against quality world opposition, but it is tough just strolling around—I can't really do it because so many people want to talk to me that I never get to where I'm wanting to go. I've almost got to lie down for two hours to prepare for a stroll at the Open, and I've certainly got to lie down after I come back. What was it someone once said—you spend a lifetime looking for recognition, then having got it you try to hide? It has happened so often, maybe not with golfers but with monied people and movie stars—Greta Garbo, Howard Hughes, Paul Getty, Ringo Starr. I understand how that can happen.

I coped with my success all right, I think. I was happy to keep coping with the pressures of a worldwide schedule until my situation changed. Compared with Severiano Ballesteros my position changed much earlier than his is changing. I was married at 22. At 28 he is still unmarried and that means he has been able to concentrate much more on his golf without any distractions, pleasant though the family distractions have been in my case. Maybe I could have maintained the high standard I achieved if I had not started a family so early, if I had not wanted to set up home in a country other than the one where I knew my main golfing objectives lay—America. I don't care for the American way of life. Neither does Seve, but Nick Faldo is finding it easier to settle there for the moment. Of course he is only two minutes old and probably has not yet encountered all the aggravations of operating in the United States. For three or four years it is OK, then it begins to get to you, unless—like Peter Oosterhuis—you throw your lot in with the Americans and show yourself happy to join them full time and live there permanently.

At one point we thought of buying a house in California but we decided against that. Much as I wanted to play golf in America the pull of Europe and home was too strong. I've been frustrated during my career on both sides of the Atlantic—in America by the general way of life on tour, and in Europe by the climate and the condition of the courses we sometimes play—but nothing in this world is perfect. I have to admit that for three or four years, as I tried to split myself between two circuits and two continents and two distinctly different ways of life, I did not know where I really belonged. The positive, go-getting part of me wanted to be in America, where I could develop, but there was a big part of me that was home bird, which meant I was happier in Europe. The home bird won, helped undoubtedly by the fact that the potential for making money in Europe as a former Open champion was incredible. If John Jacobs had not begun his expansion of the European Tour at the time he did, I think I would have ended up permanently based in the States, but I am glad it worked out the way it did in the long run.

In America everything seems so temporary. So many of the towns in the western states of Arizona and California are like massive film lots with little substance to them. You feel you could blow over a row of shops— they look as if they are made of cardboard. There is so little character about so many places in the States. It is so boring. It is a land of opportunity, of that there is no doubt, just as there is no doubt that it would never have made a satisfactory home for me.

You see the big problem was that while I wanted to play in America I also wanted to come home to dinner every night in Britain, and that was not possible. We had not reached the Star Trek era when I could have been beamed back for some good old English grub instead of the American plastic food. I loved America for the condition of their courses, and when I gave up my player's card in 1973 I soon realised I had made a mistake and got it back again in 1975. Some people thought I was being given exceptional treatment but the commissioner, Deane Beman, who, as I said, earned his own playing ticket at the same school I attended in 1967, knew I had a ten-year exemption from pre-qualifying because I was a US Open winner. I needed it back because in 1975 I was not allowed to enter Britain. I had left for Jersey and in order to take advantage of all the tax benefits I had to stay away.

So off we went back to the States—Vivien and the three children, Bradley, Warren and Tina, plus a nanny and a caddy. We travelled everywhere in a minibus. I was like a tour operator, every weekend either renting houses or arranging the hotel accommodation. We needed three rooms and it cost a fortune, but we stuck it right through the summer. I did it because I certainly did not want to be in America on my own. I have always felt that you get one shot at this life, with no second chances. When you are dead you are dead, so I was not prepared to lose the family for a whole summer. I had been places on my own before and a week seemed like a month, a month like a year—I felt so lonely. I cannot understand how a golfer like Graham Marsh from Perth in Australia can stay for six, seven or eight weeks on his own, but it is different strokes for different folks, I suppose. I'm not like that and in the mid '70s anyway the family unit was drawing my attention more and more strongly. The children were getting older, reaching that interesting stage and I wanted to be with them. They and Vivien are the greatest wealth I will ever have, far more important than money. It is important to me to take the family with me wherever I go if I can. In 1985 we were all at the Open, spending a week together at Gleneagles Hotel. I enjoy that and it is educational for the kids. They have got to see more of the world than most youngsters and by just being there they keep me from feeling miserable.

When you are battling your way to the top it is necessary to be extremely selfish and very purposeful, but I hope it never affected anyone adversely except Vivien. When we got married I told her firmly, as I said before, that golf came first in my life. I'm surprised she was prepared to take the chance but she must have sensed I had something extra and was prepared to accept those conditions. Inevitably as time went by, the golf has become less and less important in my life and Vivien and the children have taken over. She knew that would happen too. I've often thought about the selfish aspect of golf and I have rationalised it this way. You need to be not so much selfish as hard, and without too much sentiment. You cannot afford to be sorry for the other fellow. If you are, you are lost. The chances are that he will never be sorry for you anyway. It is the name of the game. Of course I disliked it when a sponsor was particularly nice to me one year and expected me as a result to be back the following season, and I didn't go because career-wise I needed to be somewhere else, but I used to try to do the right thing by people. If I made a promise there would have to be a very good reason for me not to keep it. True sometimes I saw the reason as a good one and the sponsor did not agree, but then I had to be the judge.

I have a conscience. I worry about giving a client value for money because that is my nature. If somebody pays Tony Jacklin a couple of thousand to hold a golf clinic or play an exhibition match, then they are entitled to expect a good job of work. It's my reputation that is on the line. If I didn't do a good job it would not be for want of trying, but a deal's a deal. Even if I try to do well every time I am sure there are times when the client is not completely satisfied (and some people never are), but a deal is a deal.

Fincasol, the company that built my Spanish house at cost—the house is now worth close to half a million pounds—felt they got a raw deal earlier this year when, after I'd signed a contract with them to use my name in their advertising, they were shocked that I announced I was setting up my own company with my brother-in-law to do virtually the same job. They can still use me in advertising for the next four years and I'd be happy with that. I think they should, and get their money's worth. I realise that they were hoping I could push clients their way but blood is thicker than water in this. There was nothing in the agreement that said I would not set up in opposition. A fine point perhaps but that's business. I've got a conscience, of course I have, but I've worked hard for a very long time to do the right thing and I felt that they were not quite playing the game with me anyway. They were doing business with a couple of fellows I considered I had introduced to the company but they did not tell me! Anyway there's maybe a bit of right and wrong on both sides and I hope the matter is closed.

I've worked hard for a very long time to do the right thing by the Jacklin name. I have avoided trouble and being seen in the wrong places with the wrong people. That is why the company I've formed to develop down here is called Guts, and if any of my partners in this business do not agree about the way I think it should be run to protect our integrity then either they will have to go or my name comes off the masthead. My brother-in-law and I own more than

50 per cent. I suppose that somewhere along the line we are bound to upset someone but I don't care as long as we run our business properly. I'm not trying to impress everyone. The thing I'm trying to do is operate an efficient business with standards—my standards, standards I have set over the past 20 years of meeting people, of travelling, of playing golf with top businessmen. In the long run I am interested in providing a future for my family, especially my children. That is all I am after.

When I die I hope people will say, he had his ups and downs (more ups than downs) but he was a good sort who did well by his family. If that's the legacy I leave to the world that's fine. The memory I leave behind is the soul I leave behind. I have not had too many downs but there's time yet—you never know what is going to happen. You must always be prepared for the unexpected, and I am after all only halfway along the road. I don't have any hopes for the next 40 years except for health and strength for the family. I don't want them to get hurt. Half the fun of life is that, thank goodness, you never know what is going to happen in this dumb, crazy, extraordinary world, but if this is the halfway turn for me I've got out in 31 or 32. I'm under par anyway starting for home and should be able to record a pretty useful score when the round is over. There are millions of people who have lived on this earth and died having done little, and there have been millions who have achieved a lot and received no credit, but I've been luckier than most. What I've done everyone knows about—and there is more to come.

I have sometimes been referred to as 'big-headed'. I don't know what the term big-headed means. It's an English term and you never hear it anywhere else in the world, where apparently they do not lack the confidence to give themselves the odd pat on the back. You'll never find the Americans slow to congratulate themselves about something but here in Britain it is *infra dig* to be too enthusiastic about one's own achievements. It's not cricket. In addition there is a definite group of people who resent anyone from slightly lower down the social ladder doing exceptionally well. They used to say I was big-headed because I was cocky about my potential to do well, youthfully confident about my ability to do even better. I still have a lot to be proud of, and don't mind talking about it, so I could still be termed big-headed, but it is just my normal behaviour. But you could be the most perfect fellow in the world and someone would not like you. If you are in the public eye you face up to that. I bet television news personality Selina Scott does, or Sir Alastair Burnett. They know that for every viewer who enjoys watching them on television another viewer does not, but I don't suppose it worries them too much. They just get on and do their job as professionally as they can—that is all I ever did or tried to do.

I sometimes despair about what people write about personalities who really do work hard at doing everything right. The criticism—unwarranted most of the time—surrounding members of the royal family just makes me sick. I dislike the journalism of people like Jean Rook who is looking, it seems, for the sensational every time. I refused point blank to do an interview with her once. As for the golfing press, there are good and bad like the curate's egg, I suppose. The real golf reporters I have always got on fairly well with. Inevitably during the difficult years they had to write things that sometimes I did not like, but they were entitled to their opinions, and I always tried to understand that. What I never understood, and still don't, are the hurtful pieces written by the people on the sidelines of the sport—in for one quick hit then away again.

I have always wondered why the British press are so tied to the British performances. If an Australian or a Spaniard leads a European event you can almost bet your last new pound coin that the stories the following morning will be centred on the leading British golfer. I have never thought that right, but I suppose they know their business best. Significantly perhaps, I have never kept scrapbooks although someone else did for me for a while. I don't have a whole host of the cuttings which appeared so regularly in the bad days when my putter was failing me—'Jacklin Fails Again', 'Bad Start for Jacklin'. Of course I was the only British golfer playing regularly in America at that time and I was under the microscope.

I sometimes resented the intrusion into my personal life in the days when I was right up there at the top. Nigel Dempster in the *Mail* once wrote that I was practice-chipping in Jersey when his father strolled up and offered some advice. I apparently turned to him sharply and told him to buzz off. Not only was I not chipping and had not seen his father, I was not even in Jersey at the time.

12
Friends All the Way

A great many people have helped me in my career but I'd say I have only five or six really close friends, men like Johnny Rubens up at Potters Bar. To him I was just another kid whom he wanted to help along the way. When I first needed money to go abroad he gave me a couple of hundred to make it possible—a small amount for him but a massive cash injection for the youngster struggling to make the grade, which is what I was at that time. And there were no strings attached—just a reminder to try my best all the time and gain as much experience as I could. The success I had later on made him, I'm sure, very happy to have played his part in my success story. I attended the 60th anniversary dinner of the Potters Bar club in 1984 and underlined how much I appreciated the help of everyone at the club, not least Johnny, for helping me on the road to stardom. Had I not had so much encouragement, who knows what might have happened to me. I might never have made it in golf as quickly as I did.

Johnny and I are still great friends. He wrote to me once in the early days and said that if ever I needed money there was £50,000 on deposit at a given bank in an account in my name and available for use any time. I have never needed to take advantage of it, and never will, but what a gesture. He is in his eighties now but I always try and make a dinner date with him at least once a year to chat about this, that and the other, to blow off a bit and always to listen to his highly respected opinions on various issues and situations. Now that I'm in my forties, I have got myself sorted out well enough. I know where I am going and how fast I can get there, but Johnny is always a friend who can listen and advise—and I have long appreciated this. I think it would be fair to suggest that the friends I get on with best are people in the same earning bracket as myself. It is difficult to have a close friendship with someone who has not got the means to live and entertain the way I can, because there is a barrier there, unfortunate though it may be. If you are used to going to restaurants where you know it will cost £120 for four and your mate is making not much more than that, tax paid, a week, how could the relationship, the friendship, work?

Most of my close friends are men who have made a bob or two in their day, who think the way I do, who have been successful in business and who enjoy talking golf. I don't relish lending money to people but I'd pay up willingly to a close friend to get him out of some jam or other if it arose. Mind you, I cannot imagine any of them getting into such a jam. I don't make friends easily, because I have never wanted to get too involved with people, but there's Johnny, there's Cyril Brice (who would do anything for me and me for him), Wally Dubabney, John Greetham (a farmer friend), Marshall Bellow (with whom I stay when I am in the Leeds area), and Jim Brewer from Jersey.

Marshall and I can sit and chat for hours in front of the fire (what a luxury it is having a real fire). We talk about the psychology of life and what makes people tick. Most of my friends have had the same game-plan as I have as far as life is concerned. They have worked hard to achieve success in their fields and now enjoy the rewards of that—a standard of living well above the norm. Like me they do not plan from day to day, but look far further ahead, far further than I did when I was charging around in the early and mid '70s—the period when I had less time than ever to sit and discuss with them what was happening to me. There is a stability about my close friends that I envy. Our attitudes to each other have not changed in 20 years and never will. Take Cyril Brice, for instance. He is retired now. I used to stay with him when I competed in tournaments at St Pierre Chepstow, despite the fact that the house was 70 miles away. He would drive me down in the morning while I slept and drive me home at night, after walking all the way round watching me play. He is such a nice man. I believe I have a sixth sense about people. I can tell if I like them or not from

Bing Crosby

June 22, 1970

Dear Tony:

Your thrilling victory is the greatest
thing that's happened to international
golf in many years. That was truly a
great performance.

Warmest congratulations and best wishes
for many more important victories to
come -

Your friend,

Bing Crosby

BC:lm

Mr. Tony Jacklin
1 Erieview Plaza
Cleveland, Ohio

Above: The US Open trophy (left) which I won at Hazeltine in 1970 and the Open Championship trophy I had won at Royal Lytham and St Anne's a year earlier. A rare photograph — I held both trophies simultaneously for only one month. *Willoughby Photos, Ashby*

Top right: Arnie Palmer puts his arm round me as we wait to tee off in the par 3 contest at Augusta. We played four times together in the Masters itself and seem to have been teed up in the pre-tournament short course attractions fairly often, too. Arnie won the Masters four times — I never did which is one of my great regrets. *Associated Press*

Right: Yes, that is me — in the days when I sported a 'Viva Zapata' moustache. This photograph was taken in 1973 at a tournament in Coventry. *London Photo Agency*

Above: Bradley's first set of clubs — a special cut-down version made specially for him by Dunlop.
H. W. Neale

Right: Relaxing with Vivien and our sons, Bradley and Warren.
Daily Mirror

the first meeting. I've never really found that initial reactions are wrong. I can tell within five seconds whether I want to get to know someone better or not!

I have no regrets about the way I may have treated anyone in the past. I don't have any conscience pricking me on that front. I can cut people off, like the architect Rodger Dyer who designed the house Fincasol built for me in Spain. We were fairly good friends and he did help me find the house in the Cotswolds ten years ago, and then did some work on it. We played golf together, including in the Tobago pro-ams, and generally got on well 'searching life'. Then one day we were playing tennis. It was match-point and he said a shot he hit was in. I knew the ball had not been in court, that it was definitely out, beyond any question of doubt. We had a tiff and I determined there and then that I had had enough. If he was going to act like that then I did not want to play any more. It was a stupid thing to do—and more childish than ever on my part, looking back on the incident coldly, but the relationship had been dramatically cooled. We moved away, and drifted apart, but I did not think twice about ringing him up for help with the Spanish house—he is the best architect I know.

Then there were the people in Lincolnshire who started up a car business and took my father into it as well. My father is not business-minded but he loves cars. He stayed with them for a year or two until one day they announced that they were going off on their own, without my father. I had specifically asked them to let me know if things were not going right, but they did not. They just upped and went and I was very upset. There was a distinct lack of communication, which I could not understand. In all the experience I have had with people, I find the greatest reason things go wrong—in business, in marriage, with children, whatever—is because there is a lack of communication. People keep things inside instead of speaking their mind if something is troubling them. I encourage discussion. People have told me my life is like an open book which I ought to keep closed more often to keep people guessing, but I'm not like that. There is far too much secrecy in the world today.

I have never been sorry for anything I have ever said at all—nothing. I believe in getting things off my chest, speaking up. If there is something in the way and I'm worrying about it, I talk about it with the right people. I cannot understand people who adopt a silent routine, and when asked if there is anything wrong answer that there isn't. If something is bothering me, I speak out—that is my view even if it can sometimes cause upsets. I don't mind upsetting people if I feel they have done wrong. I just want things to be right and am not afraid to speak my mind on any issue. I never doubt my actions once I have made up my mind. I might be wrong on occasions but no one will ever accuse me of sitting on the fence, of dithering or being uncertain once I have taken a decision. I am as sure of that as I am of trying to shoot my lowest possible score whenever I tee up.

Sometimes speaking my mind in the press-room has got me into trouble. I remember playing at the opening of Moor Allerton up in Leeds some years ago and commenting constructively enough that they might just have to re-lay a few greens. Peter Alliss was the tournament professional and was shocked at what I said. He raged that I should keep my comments to myself. The local paper, the *Yorkshire Post*, jumped on me for my criticism as well but no one said anything or wrote anything when later they did indeed have to re-lay a few greens. What I had said was right enough. There was no need for me to apologise for speaking the truth.

Sometimes I'm accused of being aloof because in public I don't chat all that much—but if I stopped and spoke with everybody who wanted to speak to me I would never be able to keep to any type of schedule. Anybody who knows me reasonably well would not take offence if I happened not to speak on a particular occasion. I might have been thinking about something else, or someone else, and not even have seen them—I don't ignore people on purpose but sometimes you do not realise someone's there.

Last year a company jet was sent down to Spain to pick me up and take me to an oil-related pro-am in Scotland's oil capital, Aberdeen. The whole family went with me and we had a great time. Later, after the pro-am, I was at the big dinner and noticed our pilot at a table across the way. I went over and chatted to him to find out what he had shot and left without noticing that Ronnie Corbett was sitting at the same table. I just did not see him. The Corbetts have stayed with me and I certainly did not deliberately avoid them, and I'll bet Ronnie never for a moment considered I was rude because of it. He will have been in the same position as me often enough I'm sure.

It is amazing just who you can find yourself teamed up with in a pro-am and what kind of dinner party you might find yourself at afterwards! I played the Italian Open pro-am with ex-King Constantine of Greece and ended up at his home eating caviar from a punchbowl. We told a lot of jokes round the dinner table because he has a great sense of humour.

Jackie Stewart, the former world motor-racing driver, who is another of the McCormack clients, gets involved with royalty much more than I do. I once went with him on a shoot in North Wales—a day arranged by the Rolex watch company—and there was a fair old turn out of top brass. King Constantine was there with his wife and Princess Anne and Mark Phillips, the Duke and Duchess of Westminster and the Duke of Kent, who usually presents the prizes at Wimbledon. There were so many dukes and duchesses that they had their own team. Curiously nobody has tried very hard to interest Prince Charles or Prince Andrew in golf. I once spoke to the Duke of Edinburgh about it when I went for lunch with the Queen at Buckingham Palace a few years ago. The Duke had broken his wrist playing polo years ago and golf does not interest him too much, but there is a nine-hole course in the grounds of one of the royal residences that he has a few holes on. No member of the royal family has been really interested in the Royal and Ancient game since the Duke of Windsor—the old Duke, who was nice enough to write to me when I won the US Open.

From my point of view it is nice to have met and mixed

on occasion with royalty. They all have a terrific sense of obligation to their jobs and to the country. I've never met Prince Charles but he impresses me as a really good sort, with a sense of humour and liking for a good joke or gag. He handles himself so impeccably well. I think he and the Princess, who are both under immense pressure and scrutiny all the time, do a fabulous job and they have all my respect. It's not what it might seem, being in their position. They have tough itineraries and their life is never their own.

On one occasion I played golf with US vice-president Spiro Agnew, whose golf was a big joke. He came down to Spain and the American secret service asked if I would play with him at Sotogrande. One of the original residents, George Moore, a former chairman of the American Citibank Corporation, played with us. He is 79 and he cancelled a trip to Morocco to take part in the game—which was just as well, as there was an attempted coup in Morocco that day at the place where George was supposed to be meeting the King and he would probably have been killed. Agnew was a pretty poor player as poor players go. You had to make sure you were behind him when he was driving off or playing a fairway wood, and even then you were not completely sure you were in safe territory. The security men who protected him spent more time protecting themselves during that round. He was obviously a VIP but he could not play at all. I remember calling home to England on the presidential link-up through Washington. I got through in seconds whereas the telephone service in Spain at the time was awful.

It was the done thing for presidents and vice-presidents to play golf at the time. Gerald Ford was made the first honorary member of the US PGA Tour. I played with him in the Bob Hope Classic. Technically he could play every event on tour as well as every pro-am but he took so much ribbing about his play that he has retired. Golf is a tremendous relaxation for quite a few heads of state—President Marcos of the Philippines once held up play in the World Cup in 1977 because he wanted to play nine holes with some friends as a pipe-opener and no one dared to tell him that the whole day's schedule was put into complete disarray. King Hassan of Morocco has a floodlit nine-holer in the grounds of his palace, and Kenneth Kaunda, the President of Zambia, plays golf with his cabinet on a nine-hole course specially laid out in what used to be State House. It is a game much favoured too by the stars of show business, although when I met Frank Sinatra at Biarritz we did not get to play golf. He had come down with a few friends for a holiday. I thought he was a regular guy and not a bit like his press image, which leaves a lot to be desired. He gets pestered all the time, so he would pay the hotel in Biarritz—the Palace—$10,000 to close the bar to the public and allow it to be used by his entourage. I did not manage any golf with him because I had to fly out to America the next day for another tournament. He asked Peter Townsend and me to hang back a few hours, play golf and return to White Plains airport near New York with him in his DC9, but we could not run the risk of being delayed. I regret not having done that. It would have been fun but at the time I was on the frantic golfing merry-go-round which certainly gave me little time to smell the flowers along the way.

Each year at the Bing Crosby tournament at that marvellous course, Pebble Beach, on the Californian coast at Monterey, I would play with Jim Mahoney who represented just about everybody worth knowing in Hollywood—but mostly Bob Hope. He was Sinatra's press agent for a time, which must have been a hot assignment. Later he managed Neil Diamond and Linda Ronstadt to name just two. He introduced me to a great many of the Hollywood golfing set. I remember once I was taken ill while staying at the Beverly Wilshire, the fashionable hotel in the heart of Hollywood not far from Rodeo Drive, the Bond Street of LA. Tina Sinatra, Frank's youngest daughter, came along to see how I was. They were all so worried about me—she had her personal physician come along and dose me up until I was well again.

I played golf a lot at Bel-Air, where so many of the stars play. Among my partners were Robert Stack, Vic Damone, Don Rickels, Howard Keel, Fred MacMurray and Jack Lemmon. Bel-Air was a second home to me. I was always made most welcome. Buddy Greco was also a great golfing mate, and Andy Williams too. We used to play every year in his own pro-am before the San Diego Open at Torrey Pines. They were all regular guys although Lemmon was the most nervous golfer I have ever partnered. He was ashen white, shaking and trying to appear relaxed by grinning from ear to ear like a Cheshire cat, but it only heightened the fact that he was really scared of something—playing I think. I thought he had not long to live but years later I saw him at Chasen's Restaurant in Hollywood just after he had received an Oscar nomination and he was looking much better. He was a mile or two away from a first tee of course.

Some of the stars want to play but really suffer agonies in the process. I often wonder if it is worth it to them. I wonder why they put themselves through the mental mangle. Take singer Val Doonican, one of the most relaxed men on television, rocking backwards and forwards in his chair singing ballads that can so easily lull you to sleep. I met him playing on one of the BBC Television pro-celebrity series, which seems to have been going for years without any noticeable change of format, it is so popular. The last thing the BBC wants to do with the amateurs in that programme is put them under pressure. They cut out as much of the indifferent golf as they can but Val had to withdraw because he became so tense. I played with the late Bing Crosby in the pro-celebrity the very first year, with Sean Connery and Johnny Miller. Bing was Mr Casual but on the first he missed a putt of 6in or, being charitable, no more than 9in. Bing knew he had made a real bloomer because he was a good player. He had played one year with Bob Hope in the British Amateur. The producer rather undiplomatically came up and reminded Bing that his missed putt had counted, to which the Old Groaner replied he was only too well aware of that. I thought the incident might have unnerved him, but although he was shaken he knuckled down and played well for the remaining holes in the match.

Unfortunately Bing died before his oldest son by his second marriage to Kathryn Grant, the former actress, won the US Amateur at San Francisco. He would have been so proud. Nathaniel, who has turned professional and has a European Tour card, is host each year at the Clambake—the Crosby pro-am at Pebble Beach started by his father in the '30s, but no longer run by the family. Bing was a tremendous enthusiast and he died on the course— at La Moraleja in Spain to be exact, after playing a round with a friend and the two professionals Valentin Barrios and Manuel Pinero. He collapsed as he climbed up to the clubhouse, falling and dying within minutes at Pinero's feet. Pinero recalled that he had had a good round and not shown any indication of discomfort.

While they do have the facility to cut out some of the poorer golf in the pro-celebrity matches, they are played as real. There are no retakes like in the old 'A Round with Alliss' series, where Peter—to everyone's surprise except his own—never missed from 4ft!

I enjoyed meeting all the stars because I have always been an enthusiastic film-goer. Indeed at one point Peck Prior, then President of Technicolor, and Ron Miller, executive producer of Walt Disney productions (he married Walt's daughter) played a lot of golf with me. Peck, working in London, even arranged for copies of all the latest films to be flown to me in Jersey. They were 16mm and we could have anything we wanted. We were so enthusiastic about the arrangement that he offered to instal Cinemascope in the house but I thought that was going a bit far. We had to draw the line somewhere. It is a wonder I never had a small part in a film as I was so interested in the cinema—and still am.

I did, however, have the consolation of making a record—or should I say cutting one, to use the Tin Pan Alley phraseology. It cost a couple of thousand dollars to do and it was fun although I was never any threat to the pros. On the first day I recorded my songs as for real with the full orchestra on separate tracks. On the second day I recorded the vocals on my own, and on the third day the Mike Sammes Singers came in to put the backing accompaniment on to the orchestra track and the best of my takes. The three-in-one sandwich was then pressed and released to the general public. It never got in the charts and what is worse I've even lost my copy of the record in all the moving around we have done. I still have on the shelves, however, the record Gary Player made about the same time. It was all the rage to get involved in the disc business at that time although it was the days when discs were still called records. The compact disc was a million light years away and music centres were just coming into fashion.

Sean Connery lives down in Southern Spain, and I play with him a bit, but I've never been on the set with him. I used to visit Twentieth Century Fox and watch films being made there in the huge studios opposite Rancho Park golf course but what struck me was the boredom that the actors and actresses have to cope with. There is far more tedium than glamour.

I remember one night dining at Jim Mahoney's house with, among others, George C. Scott, so fondly remembered for his portrayal of General Patten in the film *Patten*. George had come across to play in a pro-celebrity match, but he never played it. He arrived at Gleneagles and we met and chatted and I said I was looking forward to playing with him later in the week. He smiled and wandered off from the bar carrying a large vodka with a beer chaser. That was his tipple. The next morning the chap who was running the show was looking very anxious and whispered to us 'George has left'. Apparently, after a fair amount of the liquid concoction, he tried to 'phone his wife in America and couldn't. He would have had to rely, in those days, on getting the Scottish operator to connect the call, because there was no such thing as direct dialling from the depths of Perthshire. He never managed to make the connection. George showed his displeasure by pulling the 'phones in his room out of their sockets in the wall. Gleneagles, he told startled night staff, was not his kind of place, and he just walked out into the night, got into the taxi they had called and left wearing a light rain jacket. As he closed the door, one member of staff, concerned at the situation, queried anxiously what they were to do with all his clothes. 'Burn 'em' was the swift retort. The local newspaper men from Glasgow were all hovering about at lunchtime the next day but we were all sworn to secrecy. An English show-business personality was flown in to replace the big-name actor.

About three or four years after that, I was at a party in Jim Mahoney's house and noticed George reclining lazily in a hammock beside the pool. He just looked like a big teddy bear—a nicer man you would never meet, a bit overweight but looking good. Vivien and I were sitting next to him at dinner and the old white lightning began to flow again. He was into the vodka. I was naturally curious to know how he felt about acting and I certainly did not want to sit and talk golf. We were chatting about Lord Olivier when he rapped out to me that he would hear no word of criticism against that man. I had made no criticism and would not have anyway. I just wanted to know why so many actors insist that he is the greatest. Instead I got a full explanation of the importance of the theatre to an actor—the importance of playing before a live audience every night. An actor on the stage never knew how an audience would react and always had to be on his toes. Then I mentioned that Viv was from Northern Ireland and he said sharply that he did not like the Irish, and became more and more aggressive. We just accepted this and certainly were not going to argue. When the meal was over he got a bottle of brandy off the dining-room table, put it under his coat and headed off into the next room where Jim had 15 or 20 years of family portraits on the wall. He sent smaller prints as Christmas cards to friends each year. George sat down in a chair looking at these pictures with a bottle of Remy by his side and his wife watching him from a distance. She told me, when I showed a little concern, that she had her eye on him, and later wheeled him off to bed.

Hollywood living did not excite me. The bottom line was that so many people were insecure. The place was filled with people trying to get invitations to the right parties in order to be seen by the right people. It was a never-ending drive there to reach the top and, for those at the top, to stay there. The film capital of the world is kept alive by fear—the fear of being cast aside, the fear of never being discovered, the fear of losing popularity with the fans—but more importantly with the studio chiefs. It was awful. I remember

Scott said to me that he knew the way I felt standing on the eighteenth tee on the last day at Lytham the year I won the Open. If he meant that I felt apprehensive, anxious that I would crack at the last hurdle, he was mightily wrong.

Jimmy Tarbuck, Sean Connery and I have had some great games but we do not play so much these days because of circumstances. Our busiest time together was when I was just starting out in golf and Jimmy was at the Palladium. We used to be a regular pro-am partnership. Bruce Forsyth was also in our group. They are all fanatics, even Terry Wogan, who was not much of a golfer when I played with him first, but I'm sure he has improved. Tarbuck's a semi-pro, he plays so much, but for the majority of the show-biz set it is just a fun day out in the open air. They don't practise, but they can still be very competitive.

As far as I am concerned it is nice that chaps like Eric Sykes and Max Bygraves and the like have chosen my game for their relaxation, and their keenness has also meant that thousands of pounds have been raised for charities, not least the Variety Club and sports organisations for the disabled. I once went on Max's show—a Christmas singalong—and believe me I know now how they feel on the golf course. I was like a fish out of water under the studio lights. I was mighty nervous, I'll tell you. Max had had some words done on a Gilbert and Sullivan opera and I was supposed to come on and sing a bit, whack a ball, then do a routine with Max and Jimmy Tarbuck, who was also on the show. I had to learn the words and I was glad when it was all over, although I managed to look reasonably relaxed on the screen. It showed what a good actor I was! The show was recorded live before a studio audience and we did not need a second take. I realised then the pressures these fellows work under. Believe me, they work hard for their money.

The problem in Britain is that there are so few show-business stars interested in golf. You see the same names all the time in pro-ams and maybe the public are beginning to get a bit bored with it. Make no mistake, some of the show-business stars have had a fabulous life out of golf—take Telly Savalas, for instance. Kojak was so busy playing golf around the world at one stage that his schedule was tighter than mine. He used to bring an entourage wherever he played. Telly had first-class tickets from Los Angeles to everywhere. They played the King of Morocco's tournament; they played the Lancôme pro-am in Paris, and were treated royally; and they were at the old Bob Hope British Classic every one of the four years. Telly, because of the success of his detective series, was internationally known and always took a huge crowd with him when he played. He was given *carte blanche* at the tournaments and got paid whatever he wanted. Good luck to him. The public wanted to see him and he was happy to turn up. He and a lot of other stars have much to be grateful to golf for.

I remember in the Bob Hope—the first one at the RAC Club at Epsom—there were hundreds lining the fairways to see Kojak play, including a young lad who had sneaked off school to see his television hero in person. His headmaster might never have known but for the fact that Kojak's first drive was so violently hooked low just a few feet off the ground that the ball hit the little boy on the leg. Telly, of course, was over in a flash to see that he was all right—and he was—but his cover had been blown. The press photographers had the pictures, the pressmen the story. The young lad got to speak to Kojak, which was more than he had ever dreamed of, but I suspect his headmaster spoke to him the next day! Telly was no great shakes as a player but he is by no means the worst I have ever played with.

We were playing the inaugural pro-am at La Manga, the golfing complex near Alicante where Arnold Palmer once won the Spanish title. The project was the dream of Greg Peters, an international entrepreneur, and my partner was a friend of his, an important friend— one of his bankers. We played two holes and this guy had a couple of fresh-air shots, which was funny but worrying too because the format of the tournament was that the big money in the event was all tied in to the team score. I remember standing on the third hole and telling him not to worry, just to relax and enjoy it, and I pointed out that he had a shot coming up. I knew immediately it was going to be a long hard day when he asked what I meant by saying he would be getting a shot. He had so little knowledge of the game it was stupid that he was in the draw, but that sometimes happens and we just have to put up with it. I did not win! I've never played in the Million Dollar Challenge in Southern Africa at Bophuthatswana, but I'm told one of the personalities brought over to play one year was chatting to Lee Trevino and asked him what he did for a living. He thought he was the local greenkeeper! Trevino put him right and continued in polite, if bemused conversation, only to have the show-business star from Hollywood ask whether he knew or had ever played with 'Arthur or was it Alan, or was it Arnold . . . you know who!' He was trying to remember Arnold Palmer. Apparently he played so badly on the practice ground that they never let him near the first tee!

Some of the houses the stars live in are incredible. Bob Hope's at Palm Springs is built halfway up a mountain and there is a reception room as big as any in a fashionable hotel. Parties are not my scene but I went to one at Bob's. The place was packed with young starlets trying to be noticed, film producers and the millionaires who are Hope's neighbours in the Valley, and business associates. I had had enough after ten minutes and left. Hope is a superstar, and when you reach that status in America you really are hero-worshipped. They have everything they ever wanted—Hope never gets up until about 10 o'clock, when he has a daily massage—but life is difficult at times for the stars even if they do enjoy the power their stardom has brought. It is difficult for us to imagine here in Britain just how the really big stars are treated by the public—just like gods. And it's the same with the golf superstars.

It has got to the point where Nicklaus and Palmer really do believe that they are more than just ordinary people. They have reached that point because of their enormous talent but I don't envy them either, because they are scrutinised and pulled apart by the press. Everybody wants to dissect them, find out just what makes them tick or why they are so good at what they do. It's hard to remember that no matter how good a singer, a comedian or a golfer a fellow may be he is reasonably normal in every other respect. If anything goes wrong in their lives, too, you can bet the newshounds play it up for all it is worth—in those circumstances I believe the press should be more forgiving than they are. That's why in a way I have a certain sympathy for George C. Scott. I would not change places with any of them. That kind of life is too public for me. I've experienced it up to a point, yet I've never made myself inaccessible to anyone—it has always been possible to get through to me—but why is it that so often the 'phone rings just as I am sitting down to lunch or dinner? I suppose people know I'll be around then. Sometimes we just have to take the 'phone off the hook to get a little peace and privacy for an hour or two.

There are some fabulous pads at Palm Springs—on the Legends course you cannot build for less than a million dollars and even then they are strict about who they let in. I once stayed with George Glickey at Palm Springs in a house on Bermuda Dunes which was like a small hotel. He had ten cars in his garage—Rolls-Royces, Jackie Kennedy's old Cadillac, E-Type Jaguars—and, not surprisingly, he ended up building his own course. He made a million in chemicals and steel by the time he was 21, lost it, then went on to make millions more. Viv and I were very friendly with him and his wife but then she died. At one point I was going to represent his club —the Del Safari Country Club —but it all fell through.

We met so many generous people when we were a couple travelling together without a family. I'd never call the children a burden because the kids give us so much pleasure, but when they came along we tended to lead a different life. You could not go out and socialise with people quite so much. You had to stay around the hotel, to make sure the kids were all right. Then, when it became totally impractical for Vivien to travel with me, that was when I ceased to enjoy America. Then I started going for no more than three weeks at a time and even that was too long. I just did not like the loneliness of it all, but the early days were great.

13
Back to Europe

The basic problem for the McCormack Organisation, as far as I was concerned, was that I was the first superstar in British sport they had handled. In the early '70s I was making around £200,000 a year and they were making £40,000 out of that, because they take their money off the top. That was a sizeable chunk of what was needed to run the London operation then. In those days McCormack could have a team operating for that kind of money. I would be assigned a member of staff to look after my affairs—he would be dealing with others as well—but as soon as I built up a rapport with this person, as soon as I got to know him and his methods and he got to know what I liked in the way of contract-handling, it was odds on he would be moved off to another assignment. That happened on a number of occasions and whatever they want to say about it the client suffers. I definitely suffered financially from the situation because deals in the pipeline with one fellow never materialised after he left.

The toughest job a McCormack employee has is keeping all his clients happy, and basically how it works is that at the end of each year each client receives a portfolio. That is when you work out how much you made in prize money, and how much the Organisation made on the top of that for you, and most of the time I was more than satisfied. They made enough icing to satisfy my urge to get myself into a totally secure financial position for life, and I was well satisfied with the financial dealings in the short term, though less enamoured of the long-term efforts to ensure that the Jacklin name remained a household word even after I had severely cut back on tournament play.

When a new range of sportswear was to be marketed in England two years ago for Jack Nicklaus, the advertisers did a street survey to check on how many golfers the ordinary man in the street knew of or had heard about. An executive of the company who organised the survey told me I was way out in front as the golfer most well known at that time. I must in all fairness suggest that a similar poll taken today would I am sure put Severiano Ballesteros and Nick Faldo right up there as well. They are the headline-makers these days, but I have been around a lot longer. Nicklaus was second in the original poll of most-known golfers and Arnold Palmer third. The poll indicated that Nicklaus's range, given the fickleness of the shopper, would do well, but it also proved to me that I was not getting the exposure I deserved.

The MacCormack Organisation had looked after the corporate image of Arnold Palmer superbly, for obvious reasons. It had been Palmer's willingness to take on McCormack as an agent that had got the company started in the first place. These two were close friends, but in my case Mark McCormack—for all I have had many dealings with him—is just an associate, someone with whom I have been happy to work over the years in most aspects of my career. Financially it worked well, but that poll underlined that I needed to have my name on a much wider spectrum of endorsable products or to have myself involved in projects outside tournament play, exhibition matches and clinics. I wanted a broader base, but seldom got away from golf, although Viv and I once did an advert for Bisto for which Viv was paid £2,000. Sometimes I got involved in crazy projects. For instance, I once jumped on a plane for Vancouver, spent the night there, hit some balls off the roof of a new high-rise building as a publicity stunt and flew back the next day $10,000 richer. I once drove balls off the roof of the Savoy Hotel in a no-chance-at-all bid to drive over the River Thames, all to promote a new line of toy. It was daft really, but if there was money involved I did it—and that stunt made the national television news.

Of course the need to find other channels of income was not vital for me—I was making plenty in appearance money on tour in Europe. As a bonus for my assistance in playing in the various tournaments, I was permitted to charge appearance money—an issue that was later to end in a bitter wrangle between the European Tour bosses and Severiano Ballesteros, when they decided that prize money had reached a sufficient level to do away with the payment of appearance fees. These had been permitted for former Open champions and latterly the men who topped the order of merit. It was argued that appearance money was not paid in America, and in a sense that is true. The prize funds are huge there, but there are also incentive packages for many of the top players. Hunting trips can be arranged for those stars who fancy some shooting with something other than a set of clubs and a ball. Jack Nicklaus can be contracted to make course alterations or design new courses on the strength of his appearances. Payments are being made in kind all over the place, which is not surprising because the top stars are making so much money there is very little more they could be tempted with.

Here in Europe the dropping of appearance money was offset by the stars being offered lavish expenses, first-class air fares, luxury rooms in hotels and the like, but for me at the start it was cash on the nail for turning up—£2,000 a time and, later, the sliding scale operated by some sponsors if I did not make the halfway cut for one reason or another. The money was fine but everything I was earning was dependent on my turning up somewhere, on being at a certain place at a certain time to do something. I wanted to be involved in television commercials which made me money while I was sitting watching them at home, like Henry Cooper does today, but I never got the chance. I feel now I lost out on a lucrative market—although it's not too late. Henry has done remarkably well, but then he is well into the after-dinner speeches routine. He works at promoting himself and is a deservedly well-loved figure. He works harder than I would have been prepared to, certainly on the speech-making front. Although I don't enjoy it, I can get up and say whatever is required in as few appropriate words as possible if the occasion demands.

Instead of getting involved in mainstream advertising—a lucrative field ten years ago and even more lucrative now if you care to ask Patrick Allen, who used to do the advertising videos for Barratt Housing—I branched out into the ice-cream world. It was a disaster—I lost £20,000, or the equivalent of 100,000 chocolate wafers! There was a fellow who had worked with the McCormack group and gone off to the Sweet 16 company—an ice-cream franchise chain offering a minimum of sixteen different flavours, some of them spectacularly original. We had had a marvellous summer in 1976 and it seemed like a good idea to cash in on the summer trade in 1977, so along with a partner in Jersey I dipped in, hoping to cream off a useful profit at the end of the year. In fact it was an awful summer, and in addition my partner was trying—at the same time as running the ice-cream business—to run a hire-car operation. I lost heavily because I was not there to supervise, and I used the experience as a lesson never to get involved again with anything of which I did not have fairly good control. I just did not devote enough time to it. I did not give it the effort and concentration that was required to make it a success. It was very unlike me because I had always believed in the premise that you only get out what you are prepared to put in, which is why working in television advertising appears almost too good to be true. The rewards in that field, it seems to me, are always far in excess of the effort involved, because what the advertisers are buying is a name. Anyway, there is no point in crying over spilt milk or ice-cream. All I know is that the new projects I am getting involved with in Spain should be far more lucrative, or my name's not Tony Jacklin. I'll be taking a closer interest in them anyway.

There is a lot of money around in sport these days—far more than when I was in my prime—but generally there is a great deal of exaggeration on the value of contracts. All this talk of this sportsman or that being a millionaire makes me laugh. To be worth a million is a tough assignment in Britain if you are paying tax at 60 per cent. To be worth a million, tax paid, in Britain you would need to be earning at least two and a half times that amount—and that is a substantial slice of action. The papers, of course, always exaggerate. The Inland Revenue men usually keep a thick dossier on every one of the big earners. They keep tabs on us all. I bet they have a bulging file on Steve Davis or Nick Faldo or Sandy Lyle.

I'll tell you what happened to me with the tax people. About four years ago I had some tax payments pending on overseas earnings between 1970 and 1974. It was no real problem because overseas earnings in those years were not taxable in England as long as the money did not come into the country. When Harold Wilson's government changed the rules to make even overseas earnings taxable at British rates I left for Jersey. None of the money in the five-year period we are talking about was in the taxable bracket in Britain, but we met with the tax authorities to clear up what was quite obviously a misunderstanding. There were meticulous notes on my earnings and what had happened to them prepared by the tax counsel operating for McCormack's organisation. We told the tax man everything; we had nothing to hide. While we were chatting, one of the tax men said he had read a report in which I had made a reference to the expense of my house in Gloucestershire, apparently stating that it cost £500 a week to run. This was a misprint. The tax men figured that I could not possibly have run the house at that expenditure level without bringing some of my overseas earnings into the country. They had worked that out! Anyway, all my papers were in order and everything was totally above board. It was all whiter than white because that is always the way the McCormack Organisation and I would want it to be. At the end of it all, the tax men believed us, but then announced they would like a contribution anyway. I don't know why. I guess they might have been mad that I had skipped off to Jersey or something. Well I told them I was innocent of any double-dealing and that I did not owe them anything.

They had a confab with my tax adviser, and to cut the story short they said they wanted a contribution of £40,000. I put my foot down and said a very firm no. It was ridiculous. We were talking about £200,000 of income earned legitimately overseas and not eligible for tax in the UK at that time. It had been taxed anyway at source. The discussions continued and they reduced their demand to £30,000. I still said I would not pay but it was no use.

Although they further reduced their demand to £24,000 they wanted it within ten days or they would take the matter, they said, to the Appeal Court. They explained that then it would be over our heads for three years and if someone somewhere had tripped up on my figures, or said something wrong at the hearings and we lost then I could get done not only for the tax but for the interest accruing on the sum over the three years (if it took that long to be finalised). I would also be required to pay lawyers' fees equal, I am sure, to about the sum of tax we were talking about anyway. In the end I paid but I told them I had no intention of ever coming back to live in Britain permanently because I had always believed everything to be fair. I've never told anyone this before but you have no idea how upset I was.

I was disillusioned because as far as I was concerned I had never cheated once. I know there are people who enjoy the thrill of trying to pull one over the tax man (they are daft if they try) but I never did. I did everything by the book but had to pay out money I still feel they were not entitled to have. As I said, I cannot envisage returning full time to stay in the United Kingdom, which is not to say I would not have a flat which I could use on visits, especially when the children grow up. The way it stands now I am happy with the situation. I am a tax exile but the rules allow me to come back for 90 days to do my television stints, cope with the Ryder Cup and do a series of company days. The incident with the tax men shocked me. I had always had blind faith in the system but I was dumbfounded by what happened. After I won the US Open I remember saying how proud I was to be British. I put Britain right up on top. Union Jacks were flying everywhere when I took the American title—the first Briton to do so since Ted Ray in 1931. I was presented with the OBE for my services to Britain through golf. I was massively proud of my achievements; then the tax men rather spoiled it.

Severiano Ballesteros, in his first three years on tour, saved more money than I did in ten years because he lived in the right place. Spanish taxation was less punitive than British taxation. What sort of system is it that makes it more attractive for a New Zealander like Bob Charles to come and live in Britain than it is for a British player to stay in his own country? Anyway, as soon as I realised that there was little I could do about the government's policies—they were not going to change them for me—I was off to Jersey.

My average earnings for long enough were £200,000 a year, but in 1972 that was worth a lot more than the same figure today. In 1972 the pound was strong against the dollar. Today that sum would be worth eight times as much in real terms which shows how well McCormack operated for me. What they learned from me, of course, is helping them manage Nick Faldo, Sandy Lyle and Bernhard Langer more efficiently. I was the pioneer. Some of the younger players forget that the European Tour was not always the way it is today. It would never have developed as it did but for the vision of John Jacobs who saw the potential of the untapped market on the Continent and had the foresight to forecast and cash in, to all our benefits, on the growth potential. Now there are more tournaments and more prize money is on offer on the Continent than in Britain.

I played my part in helping John establish the solid operation which has been carried on so successfully by Ken Schofield. In the past three years prize money has jumped from £2 million to £4 million. When I started working with John in 1971 the fund was £400,000. Even allowing for inflation the expansion has been incredible. I was always happy to help John, who devised that appearance money scheme to suit me although nowadays appearance money is frowned upon. Winning a big Euorpean tournament brings excellent rewards—so good in fact that even those successful Europeans now working the American Tour find it well worth while to come home for selected events. When Peter Oosterhuis went to America in 1974 there was little to induce him back regularly, but it is different now for the young breed of potential golfing giants.

As I said before, McCormack' s men are not so good at fixing up endorsement deals involving long-term nationwide exposure. They fix up exhibition matches and company days expertly, often arranging massive fees, but they are not so good on the long-term deals outside sport. I have

148

talked to them about this for a number of years without any real success, although we nearly pulled off a deal with Burberrys which would have suited me fine. The deal was eventually killed at board level after everyone else had agreed, but maybe my negotiating team just asked for too much. Burberry had come out with a golf accessory line to be marketed under the general heading the Burberry Club, but the failure to get the deal clinched cost me a packet. I think I have a good name. I have worked hard to keep that good name and cannot understand why I have not been used by advertisers more for products not necessarily directly related to golf.

Financially, since 1969 I have had no worries—but my desire to lead the life of an English gent proved an expensive business in 1974. If I regret anything it was the move to Winchcombe. I was unquestionably wrong to move from a lovely house I had in Lincolnshire, but I wanted to live in the grand manner like a country squire. I wanted a stylish house with proper help in a typically quiet rural environment. We had in fact looked around for a bigger house in Lincolnshire without success. There was nothing in the Wentworth area at the time either, which was a shame because I liked that part of the country very much indeed. Then Rodger Dyer saw this massive place in the Cotswolds near Gloucester. I questioned how much it would cost to run the house, which had 33 rooms, but heating it was no problem as oil cost very little in those days—something like 2 or 3s a gallon. We had an indoor swimming pool and we kept the temperature of the water at a permanent 90°. In the end we lost £100,000 of taxed income on the house. It is the most I have ever lost on a deal and when I ran into my problems with the tax man we just turned our backs and walked away from our one big mistake. Mind you, it was a lovely old house, with a drive up to it, but these things happen, and looking at a negative situation in a positive way, I could argue that until I tried that kind of life I did not know whether I would enjoy it or not. But at what a cost!

That move was the first major mistake of my life. It was a humdinger of an error but it did not shatter the confidence

149

of my decision-making. I had been besotted by the history of the house, which intrigued me, and I wanted to be part of that history for ever, but it did not work out. You know we did not build or buy in Lincolnshire at that time because we were three and a half hours away from London's Heathrow Airport for a start, and I was doing a lot of flying at the time. Ironically there is now a motorway some two miles from the site, which runs directly into the main terminal complex at Heathrow! The journey would now take under two hours. That's life.

From Winchcombe we went to Jersey and it never even crossed my mind that I would not play much more tournament golf. I envisaged myself playing for a long, long time and not spending much time on the island in summer. Once I slowed down however, I found the island too confining. When I moved into the world of company day golf more and more, I discovered there was no room on the island to do it. There were no facilities—so I had to get out.

Jersey was a nice place and there were some very nice people, but they were bankers and businessmen and tax consultants and not the kind of people who thought about golf other than as a game to play in old clothes. They were the type who change their shoes in the car. There seemed very little inclination to develop golf there and maybe there is no real need to from a holiday point of view. The island is busy enough in the summer and in the winter, when it's cold, windy and wet most of the time, who would want to go and play there anyway? I did try to start a driving range and got as far as putting forward plans for the conversion of a field but it was turned down by the authorities. When I was leaving the island they said they had plans to provide a third course on ground below the present La Moye course and that everything was going to be OK, but it fell through as everything like that does there. The planning authority on the island is run by farmers, to whom the protection of land for farming is vital. I just found it all very disappointing, very negative and depressing on that front. At least in Spain, as things stand, everyone is positive about the future and what it holds.

14
The False Life

It used to be important to me to be liked by everyone and I used to go through life doing things which made everyone, I hoped, like me as a person; certainly I did nothing that would give them any reason not to like me. But after I won the Open and went from success to success I started getting all kinds of mail, including letters from nutcases saying that they had never liked me and even my winning the Open had not made them change their mind. They had never liked what I stood for. They said that I was a most unlikeable person and clearly would never change. These letters were, of course, always unsigned but the impact on me was considerable, even if they were only a small percentage of the many letters I received. The thing is you remember the bad ones. The fact was, I realised then, that whatever I did and however well I did it I would not please everyone. Now I make my own rules in life and if I make a good impression that's fine. I hope most of the time I do make that kind of impact but if some people get the wrong idea, take away the wrong impression, it's too bad. I try to do the right thing. I teach the children to weed their garden every night and I do so myself. I tell them to go through their day and question whether they behaved well or badly. I suppose that comes from my reasonably strict upbringing. I went to Methodist Sunday School (which I hated) until I was thirteen and some of the teaching must stick.

I believe in doing unto others as you would want to be done by them, but I know there are a whole lot of people out there brought up to comply with standards very different to my own. It is such a hostile world these days that I worry about how it might affect the children, but as parents Viv and I can only do our best to see the three of them are equipped to deal with the problems they are bound to face. I encourage all three of the kids to come home and talk problems out with us if they have any. It is important to communicate and we talk about everything with the kids—not that my parents ever did with me or my sister! I just hope the children do not get mixed up with drugs and the like but I don't think they will. They seem as strong-willed as me! I suppose the way we are bringing up our children is very different from the way I was brought up, but attitudes change.

Neither Viv nor I is deeply religious but we have our own type of religion inside us. I do believe in a God but I don't believe there is anything after death. I don't consider there is an afterlife, a heaven or a hell. I just believe in myself. I don't mean that I worship myself but I believe that my going out and doing a good job, and being nice, good to the children and to their animals, and conscientious and not lazy or idle is the way to teach others to behave. It is much easier in the long run to be good than to be bad because anybody can be bad and there is a certain satisfaction, a certain achievement in behaving well. Achievement on whatever scale is vitally important in my credo—even if it is something as simple as standing up after polishing up a club and seeing what a good job I have done.

Nothing upsets me more than lack of communication when something has gone wrong. When people say to me 'I thought you knew . . .' I get so mad. I am no mind-reader. Lack of discipline in people annoys me. I hate people who are sloppy and uncaring. To a large degree I am a perfectionist and I believe that you have to lead a disciplined life to get on—and nowhere is that more true than in golf. One of the great attributes you can have as a golfer is the ability to discipline yourself not to think about this or that, or to do the other. When I first started playing I was quite badly disciplined in myself and frequently lost my temper. It took me some time to realise that it was stupid to expend all that energy unnecessarily. Mind you, my dad said to me when I was about ten or eleven that I could not go to caddy for him any more if I didn't behave, and then later that he would take away my clubs if I ever caught me throwing one. When you lose your temper you lose your sense. I let myself down if I lose my temper anywhere, on the course or off it, so I try not to. I hate to be let down by others and never am let down more than twice by the same person. I don't mean let down on a money deal or something like that—I mean that if someone twice does not keep an appointment then I will not be messed about any more. My time is as precious as his, maybe even more so. If I make an arrangement to go somewhere or be somewhere at a certain time I'll be there.

If I do get let down I never forget. There was a man who came down here to Sotogrande who was introduced to me by one of the regular Tour caddies. He played off 6 and wanted a game, so I met him and played and we chatted. We played again and then he said he was looking for an apartment to rent for a short time. Mine was free. I don't really rent it—I keep it for family and very close friends—but I said I would rent it to him at a very cheap rate and he was delighted. He seemed a nice enough fellow but then he gradually changed a bit in character. He became quieter and one night he just disappeared leaving me with a telephone bill at the flat for £1,000. I've never heard nor seen sight of him since! That kind of thing leaves a very bad taste in the mouth. He fooled me. He said he had dreamt of playing with me since he had watched me win the Open and he fooled me. Not too many people do. Curiously I'm not all that readily available for a game. I often say no to requests from people I don't know. He got through my net!

I feel golf is such an emotional game that to have vendettas going with fellow professionals is rather stupid. To do your best at golf your game must flow untroubled by personal disputes. I don't want to be dragged into petty personal dramas that would probably make me feel worse than the other guy, even if I was right. If he committed a very minor infringement and I was not sure anyway, I'd let it go because to get involved in a scene would put me off. I'd take the view that if a player is brazen enough and cheeky enough to cheat and try and get away with it with me around they must be rather stupid and naïve. Happily, I might say, it does not often happen that I am involved in an on-course incident. I don't think many people would try anything in my company. That's good news for me because I like to get on with everyone.

I played for fun as a teenager; now I don't. Gary Player still enjoys it, still finds golf fun, because he is different in character from me, but I don't find it so. I would never go and play nine holes on my own for fun. I'd only play alone if I knew I had to get my game into shape because I had not played for a time and I needed a bit of practice before a tournament. It's sad there is not much fun left in it for me but it is a result of my having pushed myself too hard. When I do enjoy golf is when I am watching Warren, Bradley and Tina play. I sometimes start off playing with them and end up just watching them, content to drive the cart! I'm not really all that keen for one of them to follow me into pro golf. I will help them a lot if any one of them chooses golf as a career of course, and might like one of them to become my assistant, but as for tournament play, I know too much about the suffering—and I have had it relatively easy compared to some on the circuit who have never known success anywhere along the line.

We live a false life on tour. There is nothing natural about getting on and off aeroplanes and going around with the same group of fellows, week in week out, to different places in different countries, playing for thousands and thousands of pounds. It's unreal. We are like strolling actors on a stage tour—it is a strain all the time. We are always on show. It was great for a time but I know what it did for me. Now, because of all the charging around, I am disenchanted with golf. I maybe have been afraid to say it in the past because I was afraid that people might turn round and say I was ungrateful. I am not ungrateful, because I realise that golf has given me a standard of living I could never have achieved in Scunthorpe, but the game has also cost me a lot in effort, time and energy wasted on fretting and worrying. Thank God I have been fit and healthy most of the time—I have had no serious injuries. On tour, even if you shoot 68 today you still have to go out and score again tomorrow, and even if you win a tournament—and I did sometimes—there was always another event coming along the following week. I was on a glamorous treadmill. Nor was my worry the kind of worry or strain a stockbroker or a chartered accountant faces in his profession, which is an idea people have suggested to me in the past. Bankers, stockbrokers and chartered accountants do their thing in private, and do not have to face up each day to making a fool of themselves in front of hundreds of people. That can be hateful, as it was for me for a couple of seasons when I was not playing well.

I don't have too many other interests. I am not a motorcyclist like Sandy Lyle. I've messed and dabbled with fishing but I've never been greatly interested—I'm no Brian Barnes with the rod. I used to do a lot of shooting in Lincolnshire but not any more. Golf has been basically a total commitment for me. I like beaches and sunshine but I cannot sit in a chair and sunbathe. I like to be doing something. As for other hobbies—there used to be soccer. I played for the school team until I was fifteen, at what used to be left half. I learned to kick with both feet but I kept getting pulled muscles and other bothersome little injuries so I made the choice—I plumped for golf! I have never regretted that move.

I am a reasonably easygoing chap, although it takes me 30 minutes to simmer down after a bad round—maybe longer now—if I've metaphorically gone to hell and back in the four hours out on the course. Generally I am not a moody person unless I get very tired. Then I am grouchy. I need a lot of sleep. I like things the way I want them and I'm always sure the way I want them is the right way—not just for me but for all of us. I cannot stand mess and untidiness and that sort of thing, shoddiness in kids who don't brush their teeth and clean their fingernails. I do like getting my own way in family situations. I am the one who makes the decisions and Viv likes it that way. I would not go and tell her how to decorate the lounge but I would certainly want to place the pictures. I'm not very good at going to cocktail parties and small-talking to people standing around and wasting time. I am a practical person yet a bit impetuous, although never on the golf course! I could never have afforded to be. The sooner you realise your weaknesses the quicker you become a better player. That is the joy in becoming a good golfer. You learn to know yourself what your weaknesses are and how to compensate for them.

I'm in my element doing things with and for the kids. I've been married 19 years and Viv and I like doing things that are important to us. We like to get the house right and if we ever have a dinner party it is a small group of six or eight people, all of us having a good chat. I like to hear other people's views and if I think what they are saying is stupid I'll say so, and in the same way I'd expect people to tell me if they thought what I was suggesting was ridiculous. Mind you, I don't often find people so open as I am about things.

I like to discuss worthwhile things that affect the way we live or might make a difference to the way we live. We have just one shot at life and we are here only for a few years. We might as well try to get it right—imagine wasting a great part of your life because you didn't know what you were doing, how to do it or where you were going and why. There is nothing I enjoy more than a good involved talk about life and living, dissecting situations. If the conversation and the company is stimulating I'll lie awake at night in bed thinking on about it, and curiously I don't mind that. I enjoy exercising the brain. I hate having a houseful of people—30 or 40—all getting quietly drunk and burning the carpet with cigarette stubs. More than half the people in the world appear to think that that is fun but I don't.

I am a bit of a male chauvinist and I don't mind admitting it. I understand a career woman's thinking and appreciate that some women would prefer to have their own careers rather than looking after a husband and family, but if a woman wants her independence she cannot have it both ways. It has to be equality all the way, not just here and there. Deep down, I suppose I do believe in the old-fashioned way that if a woman loves a man and a man loves a woman, then the man should go out and earn and the woman should take on the responsibility of running the house and seeing it is kept properly and all the rest of it. That might be old fashioned but that is the way I see it, and in the case of Viv and me it works.

I have a marvellous wife whom I love very much indeed. I take care of her well, I hope, and will continue always to do so. There is nowhere in the world she would have liked to go to and has not been. She has never wanted for anything, even in the early days, and she has been one massive help to me in my career. It has, I'm happy to say, been a very successful marriage. It works well for us although I can understand it would not work that way for other couples. We're happy and that's all that matters. If Viv says tomorrow she wants a Rolls-Royce I'm in a position to get it for her. As far as the golf was concerned, the greatest thing Viv did was keep things normal and ticking over back home. She likes the same things as I do even to the extent that we might both order the same meal in a restaurant, and if I mix a drink it's odds on she'll just ask me to make up one of the same for her. That's the way we are. I think things out a lot before I take the final decision. Viv would say that while I'm so positive on major issues I dither a bit on the minor ones, before I finally make up my mind!

I try not to get too involved with people I don't know. I remember reading how Test cricketer Ian Botham got involved in a scrap in a pub in Scunthorpe and how he had asked what he was expected to do—stop going to pubs? I thought to myself he should have known that stardom forces you sometimes to give up things and going to the pub is one of those things. You just cannot have everything in the world. Where is the first place anyone would pick an argument with you anyway? The pub . . . I stopped going out drinking twenty years ago as soon as my face got well known. I have always had the feeling that somebody was going to come up and start an argument. This is why I don't go into the clubhouse either these days. I don't want my day spoiled. I am very sensitive about things like that. I remember a bloke came up to me in the Marine Hotel at Troon in 1973 when I was walking through the lobby with Lanny Wadkins and Tom Weiskopf. He had a very red face and white hair and he stopped me to tell me that he used to like me but no longer did because I had got such a big head. I was stunned. I said I was sorry he did not like me, that everyone was entitled to his own opinion and excused myself. Then he rapped out that he did not like the way I was cutting him short so I turned on him, told him I did not know what he was looking for, and asked him if he was just trying to annoy me. I told him I did not like being insulted when I was with friends. Weiskopf was hovering in the background in case there was any trouble. He was an oldish fellow who had had a drink or two but the incident spoiled the whole night for me. I have only stayed in a hotel at the Open once since then—at Turnberry in 1977. That incident at Troon is typical of what would happen if I went into bars. The fellow that night at Troon was probably drunk and may have regretted his actions the next day but the damage had been done. I had been upset. I take that kind of incident very seriously because I really do try to do the right thing, regardless of how it might look sometimes.

I'm very conscious of being in the public eye. If somebody asks me for an autograph I'll sign it. I always try and put best wishes down as well if I have the time. I feel I have a responsibility to the public to do that, but if it has been a big event with a lot of people watching and I've been nervous (as I can be) I sign some autographs and then disappear. I have to get away because I need some time on my own. I love having people around, but don't we all have those moments when for a short time we want to be on our own? I don't think that's exceptional. I think everyone in life has to do things as best he can to keep a social balance. If you work in a factory at a lathe all day, then you look forward to the tea break, lunchtime and getting down to the pub at night to see people and chat. That's the way you unwind. Golfers are different. They are with people all day at work and like to be on their own in the evening. When a golf star closes the door of his hotel room in the morning to go to work he is public property whether he likes it or not. Until he is back in his room later that day he is performing.

Trevino is the greatest showman of all—extrovert, full of gags, laughing all the time—but he is quite a different person in the evenings. You cannot get through to him and he is far more serious. He wants his privacy respected— and you can bet it is.

15
Superstar Colleagues

It does not take a great deal of effort to be nice to people. If a kid comes up and asks for your autograph and says simply 'Sign that', and I do and he walks away without saying thank you I'll call after him sarcastically 'You're welcome'. I just remind people like that I am a human being too, and not just an autograph machine, but it's no effort to sign. I'd like a pound note for every autograph I've done in the past 20 years.

I've had an army of fans in this country for years—not, maybe, as big an army as Arnold Palmer's in the States, but a loyal band of fans who have followed my career with interest. Some still write to me and it's nice to get their views but it is not always possible to answer every letter. It is the kind of thing I would want to do myself but I am so busy that it would be impossible. Sometimes on the course fans pluck up courage to speak and I'll usually try to chat while keeping on the move but I do draw the line at replying when someone shouts over a cheery 'Hi Tony!' just as I'm about to putt or when I'm at the top of the backswing. Generally such behaviour would be unusual because British golfing crowds are among the most knowledgeable, most sensitive and well behaved of any in the world. Don't take my word for it—Jack Nicklaus thinks so, Arnold Palmer does and so does Tom Watson. We cannot all be wrong. In America the crowds are boisterous, noisy, impolite at times. They will walk behind you as you swing, they will chatter as you putt and generally cause far more distractions than British crowds do. I had to learn to cope with that because American crowds will never change. They are out for a good time and determined to have one—whether the golfers like it or not. It's grin-and-bear-it time over there.

I never really had a hero in the early days but it would have been difficult for me to have ignored what Arnold Palmer was achieving in America, and what he was doing here in Britain at the Open. I agree with the view expressed by Hubert Green, the former US Open champion, who said a few years ago that he felt no one on the US Tour would quibble at giving Arnie 25 cents of every dollar they earned, because it was Palmer who sparked off the golfing boom. It was his charisma, his personality, his golf that suddenly attracted sponsor interest to the tune of over 16 million dollars a year, which is what they now play for in America. He is doing the same for the US Seniors Tour now. In less than five years the prize money has jumped to four million for the over 50s. His influence on the game has been staggering, but despite Hubert Green's view, Arnold certainly does not need the money. He is worth seven million dollars a year in taxed income. His empire is huge, encompassing all manner of high quality goods, each of the deals closely vetted to make sure they measure up to the Palmer image. There is never anything shoddy about anything Palmer does or recommends – indeed five out of six products put forward for his possible endorsement each year are turned down as unsuitable. It was to Palmer that Mark McCormack went some 25 years ago with the proposition that he should manage his affairs. Palmer accepted, and from that grew the massive International Management Group whose young eager executives are managing players, running tournaments, and more importantly, making money for the company in every corner of the world.

There has been some suggestion in the past that I did not have the best of relationships with Palmer, but this is not true. It may have stemmed from the fact that I have been quoted as saying that playing with him in tournaments could be a disadvantage, but that was through no fault of his. Let me try to explain what I mean.

When I went to the Masters in 1967, I was drawn with Arnold, and was very nervous about playing with him. To be truthful, I lay awake half the night wondering how I would get through the first round. He was, after all, every-

Top: George Carr of Dunlop (back) with Viv and I and Daphne and Bill Shankland, my first boss.   *Dunlop*
Above: Princess Anne seems to be enjoying the joke even if Jackie Stewart has reservations!   *The Standard*

The 1981 Open at Los Angeles.   *Lawrence W. Levy*

Above: Jack and I when we captained the Ryder Cup sides in 1983. *Daily Express*

Left: Seve Ballesteros and I looking glum at the final result of the Bell's Scotch Ryder Cup in Florida in 1983 — we lost by a point after leading all day! *Daily Express*

Viv and the children — Bradley, Warren and Tina — on the move from Jersey to Spain. *Daily Express*

body's hero. I need not have worried. Without going into detail, I played above myself, shot a 69, and outscored him by four; but I felt I was there to make up the numbers—made to feel that way by the people in the gallery not by Arnold.

Managing to come through that test did a tremendous amount for me mentally, but playing with a legend, because that is what he is, is always difficult. We played a lot at Augusta, because Clifford Roberts, who ran the tournament up to his death six years ago, believed that Arnold and I were a marvellous two-ball. Four years out of seven I was paired with Arnold, and had to contend with the extra pressures of coping with his huge army of supporters interested, let's face it, only in what he was doing. Arnold's fans don't care for, or give a great deal of consideration to, whoever is Arnold's playing partner for the day—it is just the way they are. Of course like any great personality, Arnold has his own pressures to contend with, so let's not forget his side of the story. Sometimes he must put himself above certain things in order to cope with those pressures which is fair enough; but I would have to say that everyone in a tournament should be entitled to a fair shake, and those playing with Arnold in the old days often did not get it.

That's not being unkind to Arnold. It was not his fault. It must have been just the same for players a few years earlier who were drawn with another golfing legend, Ben Hogan. Coping with the tournament itself is tough enough without having to cope with the additional tensions of competing with a golfing god!

Yet I have always got on well with Arnold in a personal sense. Life was only difficult with him on the course, although we had a sticky patch in our relationship when he was clearly upset at remarks I had apparently made, suggesting that he had never ever helped anyone. Nothing could be further from the truth. The misunderstanding may have arisen when I said on one occasion that playing with him did not really help anyone. In fact he has helped hundreds of people in all sorts of ways over the years, and still does. He works a great deal for junior golf, for various charities – indeed as much for golf and the people in it as anyone else who has ever lived. To suggest that he had never helped anyone would have been a total misconception and quite untrue.

When I have suggested in the past that Jack Nicklaus is a warmer person than Arnold I am talking, again, in a purely golfing sense, because most people would think the reverse is the case. For example, when Jack Nicklaus missed the halfway cut at the Masters in 1967 as defending champion, he stayed around and drove with the late Bobby Jones in an electric buggy over the last two days. It's my belief that in similar circumstances Arnold would have jumped into his private jet, flown out, and come back two days later to put the Green Jacket on the new winner. I have had fabulous times with both of them off the course, even if they do immediately assert their authority over any given situation. I suppose that goes with being great men in their field. Sometimes it appears that they are putting people down, but you have to remember so many people want to speak to them that they develop, not a barrier, but an attitude that would have people believe there is a barrier there. It can put people off. When their defences are down both Jack Nicklaus and Arnold Palmer are great guys, although totally different in character. They are incredible men to have done what they have done over the years, coping with the terrific adulation of an adoring public that has given them both the status of well-loved film stars like James Stewart, or the late John Wayne.

Jack is like Sean Connery in character, if not in playing ability! I don't think I've ever met anybody else like Connery or Nicklaus, who have gained such acclaim around the world and become so famous but yet who are so untouched by it all. They still maintain an ordinary aspect to life and that's great. There are no airs and graces about either 007 or the Bear. I've got a lot of time for Jack and I'd do anything for him. His record is stunning, and yet he remains so unaffected by it all. I have had the highest regard for him since I first met him at the World Cup in 1966. He was the man I wanted to take over from but it did not work out that way! I spent a great deal of time with him, too, at the players' school in Florida in 1967, which was held just up the road from his home. He was a great pal of Deane Beman—they had played on the same Walker Cup a couple of times including Muirfield in 1959, just a few weeks before Gary Player was to win the first of his three Opens. Deane, Jack and myself fished a lot and got on well but then Jack likes having people around. I think he is very considerate. If he can help someone he will, but he has to cut himself off ruthlessly from the press otherwise he would be hounded all day. People find it tough to get to the Bear in his lair on US Highway 1 in North Palm Beach, so well is he protected. No one has done more than him in terms of rewriting the record books. And originally, I wanted to be better than him! Even allowing for the fact that Lee Trevino says that a superstar emerges every ten years—Snead followed by Hogan, followed by Palmer, followed by Nicklaus, followed by Ballesteros or Watson, depending on your frame of mind—there is no doubt that Jack Nicklaus is in the megastar bracket. He stayed at the top of his sport worldwide for over 20 years—a magnificent feat by any standards.

Tom Watson is OK too, although I don't know him as well as the other two. He is a different character altogether—outwardly far more serious but capable of dramatically kicking over the traces from time to time. Like Nicklaus he is a great family man. He has a pleasant personality of the Huckleberry Finn variety and wants very much to be liked, but he is definitely more of a machine than the other two. He is chasing Harry Vardon's record of six Open wins and, even in this modern era when it is so difficult for one man to dominate the scene the way the old timers did, Watson might just manage it. Time is just on his side in his bid to score more majors than Nicklaus.

When it comes to the debate about which golfer is the better player—Seve Ballesteros or Tom Watson—I plump for Seve every time. He has an extraordinary talent which I have seen mature from the days he appeared on the scene as a raw teenager being looked after by one of his three older brothers, Manuel. It is easy to look back and say 'I told you he'd be good', but in all fairness I did. Argentinian Roberto de Vicenzo saw the potential when he urged

American business manager Ed Barner to snap the Spaniard up in 1975. They have parted now—maybe not on the best of terms—but when Barner signed up Seve it was one in the eye for the McCormack Organisation, who do now deal with him on some US fronts, following the break-up of the Barner connection. McCormack, ever hopeful that he might one day sign him up, maintains a bulky file on him, ready to pounce if given a chance but Seve is jealous of his independence. He is a very mature 28-year-old who has come through the mill with the press during the months when he refused to play on because he was in dispute with the PGA regarding appearance money. Maybe he brought a lot of trouble on himself—all I know is he had a pretty rough ride in 1981 but won through.

He is tremendously popular with the lads and even more popular with the girls. At the BBC Sports Personality of the Year function last year the BBC's assistant head of sport, Harold Anderson, who is in charge of golf coverage including the Open, spent a lot of time introducing Seve to BBC ladies who seemed to appear as if from nowhere to shake his hand and be on the receiving end of one of those flashing Latin smiles. He is the greatest golfer in the world today. I know, though, how tough it is to compare the respective talents of 36-year-old Watson and of Seve, matching up their major victories which at the start of 1985 are Seve two US Masters and two Opens, and Watson five Opens, two Masters and a US Open—won at Pebble Beach when he chipped in from an impossible position in the rough at the edge of the seventeenth green, on the final day, to ditch Nicklaus, who was poised for major win number 20, over one of his favourite courses. The US Open is the major Ballesteros most wants to win now. He wants to erase the memory of that tragic missed tee-off time at Baltusrol the year Nicklaus won the title for a fourth time in 1980 with an at-the-line victory over Iaso Aoki of Japan. There is another reason Seve wants the US title. He wants to dispel the American whispers that he is not straight enough, does not have a controlled enough game, to win a US Open on courses set up sometimes—I'd have to say—crazily by the United States Golf Association. It's so tight and the rough so thick on a US Open course that golfers, I feel, are discouraged from playing attacking golf which is a shame at the national championship of America.

I believe that Seve is not only the better player of the two—himself and Watson—but also that he gives the public better value for money. He is massively entertaining to watch, and has a range of shots that I think is more versatile than Watson's. I watched them both at Augusta this year in the rare role of spectator.

I would have loved to have won a US Masters at Augusta after having had a good chance to do so the very first year I played—1967. I remember I was in superb form and was just one off the lead at halfway. I led for a time on the third day, but then I shot 74 and 77 to end up joint sixteenth behind that year's winner, Gay Brewer, the American with the famous flying right elbow. I reckon I tried too hard on the last two days and was not ready. Roberto de Vicenzo—what a true sportsman and gentleman—ought to have earned a play-off with Bob Goalby a year later but lost by a shot after signing for a figure higher on his card than that which he had actually taken. It was his fault. A player is responsible for checking the card marked up by his opponent. It was one of the saddest sights in golf as he sat bravely trying to keep himself under control as he realised a technicality had perhaps cost him one of the coveted green jackets that go to every winner, and a place in the famous Augusta clubhouse's upstairs champions' locker room. I suppose in 1967 I was pushing my luck thinking I could win. I remember Roberto telling me several years later 'You cannot win before you play'. Roberto is such a wise man. After I won the Open he said he was glad he was not me. 'All your life now you will be like a boxer,' he said, taking a fighter's stance. 'Drop your guard and someone will hit you on the nose.' How true! In 1979 at Lytham Roberto advised Ballesteros to just go out and play for the Open title with his heart—he did and he won.

People often ask me whether I am saddened at not winning the World Match Play title at Wentworth but I don't rate that among the majors, even if five-times-winner Gary Player does, and Seve Ballesteros, three times a winner in

165

the past four years, considers the event very special. It was a wonderful concept thought up by that man of many ideas, Mark McCormack, but it is a fill-in event. Who can remember who won it four or five years ago? Who ever forgets the Open winners? No, the US Masters was the only other title I would have loved to collect. I keep getting invited back by the organisers—it is Hord Hardin who is now in charge—and I normally have too much on in Europe to accept, but I went this year to look at some of the US players who will be in the Ryder Cup. The town had changed a lot, but not the club.

Eleven years on from my last competitive Masters, I admit I enjoyed driving down Magnolia Lane again, and smelling the flowers and drinking in the atmosphere of the plushest staged event in world golf. It is all class there, to the extent that they do not even have a glossy 2in thick programme on sale. At the Masters they have a draw sheet and that is all. And they do not let anyone pay at the gate after the practice has been completed on Wednesday night. From then on it is strictly all-ticket and the tickets are like gold dust.

The figures for viewers watching the Masters telecast are enormous each year, and later in the year millions watch our Open around the world, as it happens, thanks to the advances in technology that make that possible. I am happy to be involved full time with the BBC unit, working with the very experienced Peter Alliss. Peter is very much the man in charge, having taken over so effectively from Henry Longhurst as main anchorman. Henry was a superb television personality, one of the few on television who never talked a load of drivel. I have only dabbled at television in the past but I hope this first year I have been able to highlight the mental problems that golfers have to face up to in their rounds. I have tried to analyse what is going through their minds, especially when lining up a tricky putt. Peter, like me, also had problems with his putting, prompting a premature retirement from the playing of the game, so I reckon we can both talk buckets about that—and with feeling!

I think, all things considered, everything has worked out

well for me. At 41 I'm reasonably happy to be changing tack and going off in other directions. I honestly don't think I would have enjoyed playing main-line tournaments for another five years—20 years on the road is long enough. I've had travelling right up above the top of my head. I have no major regrets except the time I wasted in the wrong area trying to get my putting sorted out. If only I could have realised then what I realise now. Of course I regret that I couldn't sort myself out but I have no bitterness.

By the time I won the two majors I knew how to play. My course management was good, my technique was solid. Each individual player just has to find out how many tournaments he can best perform in—I never did. When Seve won the Open in 1979 I sent him a short note of congratulation saying he would have a great career if he played only where he wanted to play and I underlined 'he'. I hope that may have helped him plan his schedules better than I planned mine.

We tend to romanticise golf, this wonderful game played in over 80 countries around the world by 250 million people. It is a marvellous game, a marvellous character-builder, a microcosm of life itself, but professionally it has changed so much in 20 years. When I played in my first Open at Lytham in 1963 the 50 or so writers operated from a small tent beside the clubhouse. Today 500 pressmen attend the Open, and the press tent is filled with microcomputers, video screens and instant scoring on the hole-by-hole, and there is satellite television coverage! The basic object is still the same—to get the ball in the hole in as few shots as possible—but it has grown so dramatically in a financial sense, become so commercial, that it is breeding a new type of pro—an automaton, a golfing machine who cannot afford to be too human in case he loses out financially. When the stakes are so high, personality has to be so carefully controlled to avoid making costly silly mistakes on course, that the game is breeding a new plastic-style personality about as warm and human as a bank card. It is a shame but it is as a direct result of the growth of the game that there seem to be fewer personalities about, fewer fellows willing to take a chance now and again, be different from the crowd.

They have too much to lose, unless you happen to be a Fuzzy Zoeller who just happened to marry an oil executive's daughter—with oil wells of her own. He can adopt that couldn't-care-less attitude at times, or appear to at any rate, although he tries desperately hard most of the time.

As a television man I hope I have been able to bring to life some of the less extrovert golfers. It has all been a new challenge.

16
Ryder Cup Excitement

I cannot remember what position I finished in the Ryder Cup order of merit to qualify in 1967 for what was only my second trip to the States. I had been there in 1965 for the Carling World Championship at Pleasant Valley in Massachusetts. I remember being so excited, going to America to play for my country against a team captained by the great Ben Hogan. Dai Rees, that big-hearted Welshman who died two years ago, was captain of our side, just as he had been ten years earlier when we won the match at Lindrick—the match I, as an eager teenager, had watched from the sidelines. Now I was part of the action. Dai paired me with Dave Thomas, another Welshman, who had lost the 1958 Open championship in a play-off with Peter Thomson, the five-times winner from Australia.

Thomas was a great big fellow with a heart of gold and a massively impressive long game. He had huge shoulders and used them to hit the ball prodigious distances. His golfing weakness was his wedge play. His chipping was notoriously bad, to the extent that he definitely got a complex about it—if I got obsessed later with my inability to putt, he suffered the same way because of his chipping. Anyway, we turned out to be a great partnership because our games complemented each other's. I had to hit the first tee shot and, I can tell you, coming as it did after the flag-raising ceremonies and the anthems I was particularly nervous. Needless to say, my ball went sharp left as I tried—and failed—to control my feelings and keep myself composed. I had swung too fast. After that I settled down and Dave and I won all but one of our games. We beat, lost and halved with Al Geiberger and Gene Littler, two players who battled bravely in later years with illness, and beat Doug Sanders and Gay Brewer in another match. Our personal battles with Geiberger and Littler were a feature of that match. Indeed Dave also played Littler in one of the singles and they halved. I lost in my singles to Palmer and to Gardner Dickinson, not one of my favourite men.

Team captain Rees had decided that in order to ease the pressure on Thomas's chipping I should drive at all the odd holes which, conveniently, at the Champions Club in Houston were par-5s. That meant Dave would have the tee shots at all the par-3s because they came at even holes. It seemed a sensible arrangement. At the short holes if Dave did miss the green I would be chipping on, and at the long holes if Dave did not get up in 2 I would again have that wedge shot he dreaded so much.

I must say I did feel the pressure of playing for Britain. It was just Britain in those days—the way Samuel Ryder, the Lancashire seedsman who first backed the two-yearly competition originally envisaged it, although Continentals are now involved. It was not the first time I had been a representative golfer because I had played in the very early days for England's boys' team and for England again in the World Cup in Tokyo in 1966, but there is and always will be something special about the Ryder Cup, now sponsored by the Bells Scotch whisky company who, clearly, have an eye for tradition. Everyone expects you to do well in the Cup—it is the big one. It's definitely a 'for Queen and country' situation. I know I felt very proud. Dai was a good captain and I liked him very much indeed. I was the new young fellow in the team and he looked after me, although I was too young to analyse closely his captaincy technique. He had a simple enough philosophy. He just did as best he could to pair golfers whose personalities and games suited each other, and he tried to imbue us with some of the tremendous enthusiasm which characterised everything he did—including being a supporter of Arsenal football club. He was one of life's great enthusiasts and so supportive of the team. Little did I think then, eighteen years ago, that one day I would be in Dai's role, trying to inspire my team the way he did us.

Only one thing upset me on that trip—an unofficial ride in a jet plane with Arnold Palmer and Scotland's George Will, the highly successful club pro at Sundridge Park for the past 20 years. Arnie, proud as a peacock, had come up to us on the practice ground and asked us if we wanted to have a flight in the new Lear jet which he had just acquired. (Now he has two!) We jumped at the chance, even though George was a notoriously bad flier. Up we went, and Arnold who could, of course, pilot the thing frightened us to death. He got up to some awful aerobatic antics to prove what the plane could do. He was like a kid with a new toy. At one point we were doing 500 miles an hour 200ft off the ground. George was more frightened than me but I was ashen white. He was green. That gives you some idea of the way we felt. I will never forget that flight and I'm sure George won't either. It did nothing to make him any less apprehensive about flying.

George Will at that time was the young golfer of whom much was expected. He had a very sound method and he looked the part but he eventually opted out of the American scene for personal reasons. His then wife did not want him to go to America on a more permanent basis—and he didn't. Generally, and quite rightly, not much is written about the role of the wife, but her attitude is very important in shaping her husband's career. No names, no pack drill, but one golfer who for a time was a regular on the Tour ran into so much hassle at home that when his wife gave him the ultimatum—choose between me and golf—he chose golf and is now happily remarried with a wife who is much more understanding.

It is not conducive to a relaxed performance on the course if your wife, with you on tour, is clearly not happy, not enjoying it, bored, and maybe even downright hostile to the lifestyle. I've been lucky. Vivien has always appreciated that whatever we have achieved in our life is down to golf and my ability to play it, for a time, better than anyone else in Europe, and for a spell better than anyone in the world. Golf has afforded us the luxury of living well. Vivien has always accompanied me whenever she could and she has walked and watched me play most rounds. She is a total fan and a very understanding one at that. Fortunately she is genuinely interested in the game and now, as the children have grown up, she is playing much more with her own circle of friends. They have a great time playing their own competitions. Of course now that I'm based in Spain she has the opportunity if she wishes to play almost every day, and her golf is improving by leaps and bounds. I must say that on tour I loved to have her along. I always have a good time when she is there, far better than if she is not. She knows how to handle me irrespective of what I score—not that I think I am all that difficult. Frankly she knows the professional game so well that when she came to play the game herself I expected her to know all about the amateur scene too, but of course she did not.

She has watched me so much that she can spot whether I am swinging correctly or not, whether I'm swinging too fast or not. She knows little or nothing about her own game, however, and how it works—but she is a keen competitor. Maybe some of my own determination has rubbed off on her. Like me she likes winning—and that's not a bad thing even if it is un-British! When she walks round watching me play she knows when something has affected me and helps me put it into perspective later—not that we discuss golf very much. It is just my job. Our discussions when I was more closely involved on the circuit centred on planning the schedule, working out how much time we would have at home, where we would like to visit again. To be frank, indeed positively blasé, there are not too many places we've not been to that we would like to go. I suppose maybe Egypt, to visit the pyramids, not that I'm much of a tourist. Not many of the golfers are! I've been in Rome many times and never been in St Peter's Square, which I suppose must seem awful to people who have longed to go to Rome and have never got there. We are wherever we are to work!

I've done so much travelling in the last 20 years, climbed up so many aircraft steps, drunk so many cups of airport tea and coffee, carted so many cases and golf clubs through those endless corridors in the international air terminals of the world, that I would not care if I never got on an aeroplane again and never went near a terminal. I like being at home. Even when, as happens from time to time, I am offered two first-class tickets and superb appearance money for Viv and me to fly off, I'll mull it over very carefully in my mind and will just as likely turn it down, although in 1985 I went down to play in the Nigerian Open. That was not too bad because the time change from Spain was nothing but on the long flights out to the Far East and Australia, where the time change is as much as ten or eleven hours, well that's a killer for me now. But I was talking about the Ryder Cup.

I never got on with Eric Brown, the Ryder Cup captain in 1969 and again in 1971. Maybe our personalities were too alike. I had a relationship with him rather like the one I had with Bill Shankland. I had had a run-in with Eric early in my career, at Walton Heath in 1964 and in the old News of the World Match Play Championship. I remember I was in a bunker on one hole and I looked over to see whether it was me or him to play. He was leaning on a club mimicking a yawn and I was so annoyed I determined I would do my best not only to beat him but to paralyse him—and did. I know he didn't like it.

When he first captained the Cup team at Royal Birkdale in 1969 I was Open champion and he could not boss me around too much, so there were no major personality problems during the week but I basically did not like the way Eric laid down the ground rules. He went into that match as if we were fighting a war. He told us not to look for the opposition's ball if it was in the rough, that kind of thing. Well I ignored that request. I mean it is a game and a match of honour and the only way to win is proudly knowing you have not succeeded by default. I refused to adopt the captain's policy and thank goodness I was not involved in any of the incidents that week—unpleasant enough incidents which detracted from the spirit of the match as envisaged by Samuel Ryder. There was trouble between Brian Huggett and Bernard Gallacher in their game against Dave Hill and Ken Still but the long and the short of it that year was that, whether I agreed with Eric's attitude or not, we got a draw—the best result for us since Dai Rees' team had won in 1957.

I always remember Eric walking down the eighteenth on the final afternoon, hands in his pockets, trying to look relaxed when he was as tight as a drum. He sidled up to me and told me what I had to do, as if I didn't know. I needed to halve with Nicklaus to force the draw. It was desperately close—just the kind of a situation that inspires Jack, and excites me. I was Open champion and the pride of Britain rested on my shoulders. I had holed a monster putt for a winning eagle on the seventeenth after Jack had played the hole copy-book fashion for a birdie he was sure would get him at least a half. He had hopes, I think, of even winning the hole, the game and the match there. Anyway, I sneaked one in and we were all square in our game, and all square in the match, and thousands at the course, with thousands more watching on television, were about to see one of the greatest acts of sportsmanship by anyone anywhere. As we walked up the eighteenth, Jack asked if I was nervous. I said I was, and he helped me a lot by saying he was too.

Jack and I both hit the fairway and we both hit the green. I putted first and hit it to 2ft. He had a putt to win, and from 15ft, with the adrenalin pumping, sent it 4½ft past the hole. Now I had a chance of winning the game and the match, if he missed and I holed what I knew was a short putt but a tricky one in the conditions. Jack promptly rolled his in for a 4 and I was left with mine. Imagine my astonishment when Jack stepped forward, picked up my marker and said 'I don't think you would have missed that one'. My heart was beating furiously. Nothing is ever certain in golf. Of course it was unlikely I would have missed but I could have. Jack continued, 'I'd not give you the opportunity to miss it'. I'd beaten him 4 and 3 in the morning and halved with him in the afternoon and the match was all tied up. It was a marvellous moment for me, for the team, for Eric and especially for the game, but Sam Snead, the American captain, was not happy. He did not subscribe to Nicklaus's gesture, a gesture he felt probably cost the Americans another victory. Yet that did not matter. Jack did what he thought was right at the time.

I've often thought what I would have done in a similar position had the roles been reversed. Of course it is only conjecture but I would like to think I might have been as magnanimous as Nicklaus was on that occasion. I would like

174

to think I would have been that big-hearted, but I don't know. We don't win the match all that often and God knows what Eric would have said to me if I had conceded a 2 footer on the last! One thing I am sure about, however, is that I would never have wanted to win that day because Nicklaus missed his putt. I have often sat at matches and round greens and cringed when I heard fans whisper under their breaths 'Miss it' when someone they don't want to win comes up to putt. That makes me sick. There is no pride in winning that way. There is no satisfaction in winning because other people fall over. I dropped a note off to Jack later just reiterating how much I appreciated what he had done—not for me but for golf. His action was spontaneous and remarkable.

The satisfaction is in playing well enough to win, like I did at the Open when everyone tried desperately hard to catch me and no one did. I won not because someone took 6 at the last to let me in but because I played strongly right to the end. Another magic moment for me was winning the Lancôme in Paris in 1970, when I knew I had to finish eagle, birdie to beat Arnold Palmer. The seventeenth is a long uphill par-5 but I hit the green that day with a drive and 4-iron. I've never hit the green again there and goodness knows how many more times I have played the hole. That year in the Lancôme I hit two of the most enormous shots I've ever hit in my life and then sank the 16ft putt for the eagle. Coming down the last I drove safely, wedged over the lake to 8ft and rapped that one in to win. I beat Palmer and Spain's Ramon Sota, the uncle of Severiano Balles-teros, and knowing what I had to do and doing it provided satisfaction beyond belief.

Seve must have felt that same way when he made his 4 at the seventeenth, the Road Hole, at St Andrews last year and then birdied the last to shake off the challenge of Tom Watson and Bernhard Langer to win the Open at the home of golf. Watson himself had no doubt felt that great upsurge of satisfaction when he hit his drive and cracking 2-iron on to the green at the last to win the Open at Birkdale the year before. That was far more satisfying for him than winning the way he did at Troon in 1982, when everyone who

175

challenged him backed off. I still feel great, too, when I think of the 3-wood second shot I hit on to the back of the green at the exposed Torrey Pines course in San Diego in the Open there in 1970, when I tied with Pete Brown. That shot nearly hit the pin and the subsequent two putts were right out of the textbook, but sadly I did not go on to win that time. Brown won at the third extra hole. For me it is the same in match-play—I'm not looking to win holes because my opponent makes a mistake, I'm looking to win them because I play better than him. I played a lot of match-play when was young, but then less as a pro. When I did play as a pro I was the target, the man to beat. My opponents had nothing to lose. I always tried to play my own game and if I won I won and if not, well it was too bad.

In that Ryder Cup match in 1969 I played so well that I was sorry there was not another major title event scheduled the following week.

Eric was again captain in 1971, when we travelled to St Louis in Missouri to play at the famous Old Warson Club in temperatures and humidity readings both in the hundreds. It was a sauna bath but again we all played well, even Neil Coles who, because he does not fly—he had a nasty experience once when landing at Heathrow on a flight from Edinburgh—went by boat and then drove from New York. Eric and I had a bit of a set-to early on. Having won the US Open by this time and being a regular on the American Tour I had made something of a name for myself. Of course when we arrived at St Louis the press fellows, some of whom knew me anyway, sought me out for comments. I was aware that Eric was captain and should be spokesman and suggested they talk to him but inevitably I was surrounded for quite some time. I said the minimum I could. I just tried to be polite. I don't know whether Eric resented the attention I was being given or not but by the time I had finished not only was he unhappy but there was no room left on the bus that was to take us to the course.

As Vivien and I stood outside, a chap came up to say he had a Rolls-Royce like mine at the airport and he could drive us to the hotel if we wanted to join him. I was not sure about this. I said we should really stick with the team but I checked with dear old John Bywaters, the then secretary of the PGA, who readily gave his approval. It seemed logical since there was standing room only in the coach anyway. When I got to the hotel Eric was reasonably short with me. He did not, he said, want me riding in Rolls-Royces when he and the team were going by bus. I explained that it had not been my fault but was not prepared to argue about it. I suppose I agree in hindsight—he said what had to be said. It was probably fair enough, but there were extenuating circumstances. How things have changed nowadays, when the team flies in from every quarter, making their own way and simply ensuring they are there by the deadline.

I played three times with Brian Huggett in that match, losing once, winning once and halving once. I chipped in at the last to halve a first-day second-series foursome with Lee Trevino and Mason Rudolph, which was ironic when you consider what Trevino did to me a year later at Muirfield in the Open! I lost both my singles that year on the last green to Trevino and to J. C. Snead, the nephew of Sam Snead, but then my record in Ryder Cup singles was not good generally. After 1969 when I won 1½ points out of 2, both against Nicklaus, I only won 1 point out of 5 in the remaining singles I played. I never could quite get going. I don't know why—maybe I was just too locked into card-and-pencil play.

The 1971 match was the year John Garner made the side and played just once, but that was one more time than in 1973 at Muirfield when he never got selected to play in four-balls, foursomes or singles by the new captain, Bernard Hunt. I remember that Peter Oosterhuis and I watched him practising at St Louis and noticed he was taking the club back too far on the inside. Separately and unbeknown to each other we told him, but he told us he did not need our help and that he could figure out his own problems.

There was an incident in 1971 between Arnold Palmer's caddy and Bernard Gallacher's that ended up with our losing a hole we should have won. Gallacher, always such a great Cup battler, and Oosterhuis were playing Palmer and my old friend (and I use the word sarcastically) Gardner

177

Dickinson. Unbeknown to either Palmer or Gallacher, Gallacher's caddy—an American—asked Palmer's man in a whisper; before Gallacher had hit, what Arnold had hit to a certain short hole. The answer did not affect Gallacher's club selection because Gallacher was unaware even of the conversation, but Dickinson was in like a flash to complain about this matter to the referee, who awarded the Americans the hole, when we were lying far closer to the stick. It was a case of the letter of the law overriding the spirit of it, and I wish the referee had been a little more charitable in his interpretation of the rule.

I was always afraid of getting involved in incidents in match-play, where everyone is hypersensitive about the rules because we seldom played match-play. There are differences between stroke-play and match-play rules and it is easy to trip up. I was always glad when a match was over without any unpleasantness but I'm afraid there was some bad feeling in 1971.

Two years later, in 1973, at Muirfield we thought we had a good chance, but Bernard Gallacher became ill and team captain Bernard Hunt's pairings were thrown into confusion. He had planned to play Bernard with his World Cup colleague Brian Barnes on the first and second days, but could not which was a shame. The Scots had taken 2 points on the first day. I had struck up a partnership with Peter Oosterhuis, and on the first-day four-balls we were in against Tom Weiskopf and Billy Casper. We went to the turn in 30 and were about 5 up. It was ridiculous really, and Casper did not like it. He came up to me on the eighth tee and asked me if I was enjoying myself and I did not feel it was necessary to be in any way diplomatic. Very much, I said, very much indeed. It's funny how little things stick in your mind about Cup matches. That was the one where Her Royal Highness Princess Margaret came to watch some of the play.

Two years later—well, it just was not our year. We lost heavily at Laurel Valley, Ligonier, and some people even suggested it was time to scrap the match. Jack Nicklaus and the officials of both our PGA and the American PGA had a better idea. They came to the conclusion that a different format—with fewer points at stake—would make the match closer, but that did not work either. The Americans came to Lytham in 1977 and found they played so little golf it was hardly worth making the trip.

Two years later, in 1979, by which time of course Severiano Ballesteros had burst on the scene, the Cup matches were reorganised again. More points were available and this time Continentals could play as part of a new British, Irish and Continental side. The switch in rules was made with the total agreement of Samuel Ryder's daughter.

Returning to that bad year for us, 1975, the match went to the home, in the Pennsylvanian mountains, of Arnold Palmer. He had been brought up on the edge of the golf course at Latrobe, sneaking on to play when the members were not around, just as Seve Ballesteros was to do years later at Pedrena. The Latrobe course was clearly not suitable but the nearby Laurel Valley was, and Bernard Hunt again captained the side—a side that found certain of the Americans in devastating form. I remember being beaten by Ray Floyd in the singles, when I was so unlucky. He played miracle golf on the last nine, shooting 7 under for the last eight holes. I tried but could not live with that. It was the Cup match where Brian Barnes was twice drawn against Jack Nicklaus. In the morning singles on the final day, by which time we had won only two and drawn three of the sixteen games played in four-ball and foursomes, Barnes won by 4 and 2 and so staggered Jack that the Golden Bear requested a return match if team captain Arnold Palmer could fix it. Technically it was not possible to arrange games like this but whether the rules were bent a little, or whether it just happened to be a lucky draw, they met again in the afternoon, with Nicklaus talking animatedly about his revenge. In fact Barnes came out on top once more this time by 2 and 1. Two wins in one day against Nicklaus was a feat that few golfers could boast about—but there was little else to be cheery about as we went down 18-8 with six halved.

In fairness, it was usually a very one-sided fixture and I was not surprised that the impact of victory that year in the American papers was rather tame. Back home in Britain everyone was getting more and more disappointed at the turn of events after the high of 1969. The Americans had such strength and depth compared to us, and their circuit was so much more competitive, that the standard of player they could field was at that time bound to be better—right down the line. As for me—and despite my record—I probably had a better chance of doing well because I had no inferiority complex about the Americans! After all, I had played against them and with them for several years and had won their major championship —but, allowing for that, in-depth class was always, it was felt, going to tell. I did not agree that the fixture should be abandoned simply because we lost most of the time. I thought, and still do, that there is considerable mileage to be gained from the intermingling of personnel from the two PGAs because—and sometimes it was easy to forget this—Samuel Ryder's Cup was put up to cement friendship between the two Associations.

The Americans, proud as they were to have the chance of playing in the match for their country, were beginning to become a bit blasé about the Cup as well. Tom Weiskopf missed the 1977 fixture back in England at Lytham because he preferred to go off and shoot a rare species of mountain sheep. That was how he felt about the Ryder Cup. His action spurred the moves to reorganise, regroup and try to make more of a match of the two-yearly competition.

In 1977 Brian Huggett had been appointed in succession to Bernard Hunt, and I'm afraid we had a major disagreement. What happened was that Eamonn Darcy and I, having halved with Ed Sneed and Don January in a first-day foursome, had lost 5 and 3 in the four-balls to Dave Stockton and Dave Hill on the second day. I did not totally agree with the pairing of Eamonn and myself because I did not feel we had a lot in common, but we gave our best and on the second day it was not good enough. It was mid-afternoon and after our match we joined Tommy Horton and Bernard Gallacher to walk back out on to the course to watch Ken Brown and Mark James, who were battling with Lou Graham and Hale Irwin. At the seventeenth we were just inside the ropes. I was walking in front with Darcy, with Horton and Gallacher behind, when Brian Huggett came along behind us in his buggy and asked me if Eamonn and I had been practising. I said no we had not been—after losing we had had a quick cup of tea and come back out on to the course to support the lads in the last match. Then Brian sounded off about what we should and should not have been doing. I was amazed.

I don't know whether it was the nerves of the occasion or not, but there were a lot of spectators within easy hearing distance of the incident and I did not like his manner. I asked to see him for a moment on the other side of the fairway, where I knew we would be in nobody's way and far enough from the paying spectators to speak a bit more freely. I turned on him and told him he had been totally out of order in his handling of the situation. I did not mince my words—I was fuming at the manner in which I had been dealt with in public. He had seemed distant during the earlier part of the week, keeping himself remote from the side, sitting with his wife Winnie at a table for two and not joining any one group. I suppose he did not want to be accused of favouritism to this player or that, but it had seemed strange to me. I told him he could not treat people like that as we had given of our best, though sadly it had not been good enough. We had tried and we had lost. I told him that he and I were finished and he responded swiftly by dropping me from the last-day singles.

We never spoke more than briefly for years, but recently we both turned up at a British Telecom function at Turnberry. We were captains of, respectively, an English and Welsh side. Seven years on from the incident we had a cool working relationship, keeping ourselves very much to ourselves socially, which was made easier because Brian had retired from full-time tournament play to concentrate on other money-making ventures of his own. Anyway, Huggett stood up at the function and made his closing speech. Towards the end he referred to our difference of opinion at Lytham in 1977 and he said he was sorry about the contretemps. I'll admit I was somewhat taken by surprise, but although I never forget, I don't harbour grudges, and when it was my turn to speak I said that I

181

thought we knew each other too well to let something like that bother us.

It has always been my policy that it is better to have friends than enemies. I do try to be nice to everyone, and to show courtesy on the golf course to my opponents. I try to be careful what I say and to whom I say it. I've not had any major rows with officialdom. I have always got on all right with most of the ruling bodies. I do remember once writing to the German Federation to query the choice of Berlin as a venue, suggesting the championship would be much more successful in Frankfurt, Cologne or Dusseldorf. I did not have to wait too long for the response—which was a courteously termed but nonetheless firm 'mind your own business'. I did, however, know what I was talking about, because the championship in Berlin, won by Neil Coles, was not one of the Federation's outstanding successes, but I guess there was a 'political' reason to take it there in 1980.

17
The Captain's Role

There is little doubt that the antics of Ken Brown and Mark James in the Cup match at the Greenbrier, White Sulphur Springs in 1979 did nothing to help team morale. We lost 17-11 that year and, looking back, I still cannot fathom out what went wrong. It was the first time that Continentals had been included in the new-style Cup match and Seve Ballesteros and Antonio Garrido from Spain were both in the team and fitted in well, but Mark and Ken were strangely out of tune with the rest of us. Knowing them as I do now I just cannot understand why their behaviour was at times so bizarre. It certainly would not happen now—I'm sure that they themselves regret it. It seemed to the other members of the side that they did not always appreciate that they were there to represent their country. They were in a world of their own. Today they are both married and have totally changed. Their behaviour in 1979 was in complete contrast to their subsequent performances.

To begin with, they almost missed the opening ceremony. Team captain John Jacobs, preferring to let his players organise themselves the way they chose so that everyone was completely relaxed, insisted on only one thing: that we all turn up at team meetings. Perhaps they mixed up the times, but Ken and Mark missed one meeting altogether. Today they would be the first there! So many times at the Greenbrier they did silly little things that were upsetting—and not only off the course. Ken, who was a very intense player then, hardly opened his mouth when he and Des Smyth played the afternoon foursomes on the first day against Hale Irwin and Tom Kite. Not surprisingly they lost by 7 and 6. Maybe Brown was upset that Mark and he had been split up after losing the morning 4 balls to Fuzzy Zoeller and Lee Trevino by 3 and 2. Maybe the pressure of the occasion had got to them. Whatever it was, it caused an unsettling atmosphere in the camp. Yet when it came to disciplining them a few months later there were members of the committee quite happy to forgive and forget. Even team captain Jacobs took a softer line than many imagined he might.

It was not his job to decide on what action should be taken but he had had to deal at first hand with the situation and some of us thought he might send them home. Yet that could have caused more controversy and certainly would have cost us two points because everyone played on the last day—a new departure. James was injured and under the rules American team captain Billy Casper matched him up with Dr Gil Morgan for a half point on paper. That was another peculiar incident! Casper was lucky not to have had to pull out Lee Trevino. Before the Cup began, each team captain was asked to put an envelope into the hotel safe containing the name of the player the captain would want to leave out if one of the other side was out of action on the last day. When it became clear that Mark could not play for us, Casper pleaded with officials that he had misunderstood the regulations and written down the name of his strongest team man. We were very accommodating about this, and it was Gil Morgan who stepped down. The outcome of the problems of 1979 was that James was heavily fined and Brown fined and banned from playing the next match. I'll admit I was mad about the incidents at the time but it is all in the past now. For 1985, all I wanted was total unity, no controversy and a winning score—and I knew I could count on Ken and Mark's support.

In 1981 I was passed over for one of the invitation spots because, it was argued, I was too old at 37! Ironically, Mark James got the spot I might have hoped for, underlining that bygones were very much bygones. A committee was set up to choose the last two spots

It consisted of Bernhard Langer, the European No. 1 money-earner of the previous year, who had never played in a Ryder Cup match, Neil Coles, the Tournament Players' chairman, and team captain Jacobs, who had his own ideas about whom he wanted in the team. He definitely wanted to get Severiano Ballesteros and reigning Canadian Open winner Peter Oosterhuis in the side, but Seve was in the black books in 1981 for arguing about appearance money. In fact he did not play for more than half the season. Jacobs persuaded him to settle his differences, promising to do his best to get him in the side. But if Jacobs wanted Ballesteros in, Neil Coles most certainly did not. As chairman he was probably angry and upset that Seve had refused to follow the official line on no appearance money, but he certainly did not want him in the team at Walton Heath. Langer tried to remain neutral, but he was aware of a groundswell of player opposition to Ballesteros just coming back at the end of the season and walking into the side. Yet Ballesteros was the best player in Europe! He did not make it. He was blackballed out of the side and the Americans must have rubbed their hands with glee.

I didn't make it either, but Mark James got in by invitation although Jacobs could easily have vetoed this. After all, James had been fined £2,000 —the highest fine in PGA history—for his behaviour two years earlier. Brown had been fined £1,500 and banned from the match, but James was eligible and although he was not able to play himself into the side, he was selected. Jacobs clearly considered that what James had done in 1979 at the Greenbrier was of little consequence. All that was forgotten in 1981, though, as James went into the side with Oosterhuis, to the exclusion of Ballesteros and myself. I have never discussed the matter with either Neil or John, and neither has ever raised the matter with me. Then I was asked if I would go along to Walton Heath as an official. I said a very firm 'no, thank you' to that. Looking back, I am still of the view that I should have been in as twelfth man, behind Severiano Ballesteros. I should have been in ahead of James, despite the fact that he was eleventh and I was twelfth in the money list when the Cup cut-off came. I should probably have been in ahead of Oosterhuis, who had quite clearly turned his back on European golf, unlike me—but then he had a big win under his belt that year, having won the Canadian at Glen Abbey and always had done well in the Cup.

Not getting in when James did saddened me a lot, and I was not surprised that Ballesteros was bitter about his omission. The problem then was that the selectors could not separate themselves and their opinions from their own involvement with players on the Tour. Mind you, that was the case in almost everything the full committee discussed. Even when it came to fixing the wages of our full-time staff, some committee men would compare the proposed wage with what they were earning each year. That was the mentality of some of them. As for my Cup omission, nothing has hurt me more in golf. If winning the Open and US Open were highlights, being left out in 1981 was one of the great disappointments. Another, incidentally, was not winning a BBC Sports Personality of the Year award in 1969 or 1970. I could not have done much more for my sport than I did in those two years, but Ann Jones won Wimbledon in 1969 and won the Trophy, and in 1970 Henry Cooper was the recipient of the award. Anyway, that is history and so too is what happened in 1981. I never wanted anything more to do with the Cup at that point. In my own mind I was finished with the Ryder Cup for ever—but it did not turn out that way.

In May 1983 the wounds had healed a bit when Ken Schofield, the secretary of the PGA European Tour, came up to me on the putting green just before I teed off in the first round of the Care Plan Tournament at Sandmoor in Leeds. Bernard Gallacher had alerted me to expect a call from Ken the evening before, but I never thought of my being offered the captaincy, although I was aware that the newspapers had been urging my consideration. I had not thought about the captaincy because I had become uninterested in the Cup after the selectors left me out. Anyway, Ken came up to me before the first round of the tournament at Sandmoor and asked me to lead the 1983 side. I did not accept straightaway. I said I would only consider it if the team could travel first class. Ken said he would see what could be done on that issue. I said that before I could say yes I would need to know the answer to that one, because I knew how many times in the past we had turned up in America feeling like second-class citizens—

hardly psychologically primed to take on the most confident golfers in the world. Too many times in the past the Cup had been run, it seemed, more for the officials than for the players. Priorities had been in the wrong places. If I was to be captain it would be run and organised with the players in mind.

After Ken Schofield's approach to me I went out at Sandmoor and shot a 65 to jointly lead the field with Spain's Juan Anglada and Howard Clark, who lived just down the road, but I was thinking about the offer. I thought again about what had happened in 1981 when I reckoned I could have done so much for team morale but was not given the chance. Yet I felt that it would be wrong to carry a vendetta that far. I did not want to be remembered as a big cry-baby because of what had happened in 1981. I knew I was coming towards the end of my career. I realised that while I was initially mad and hurt it would be a stupid thing to say no —assuming I could get the guarantees for the team. In addition, the appointment a few months earlier of Jack Nicklaus as the American team captain probably influenced my decision to bury the Ryder Cup hatchet I had been brandishing for almost two years. After what had happened at Royal Birkdale in the match in 1969, Jack and I had a very special relationship in Ryder Cup history. It seemed to make sense to accept the offer. I had had a good career out of golf and frankly I would, on reflection, have hated it to be marred by an incident that could later have been regarded as sour grapes on my part.

It seemed strange to me that no one had sounded me out earlier about the captaincy, even stranger that the first inkling I got of it was minutes before I went out to play in an event, but anyway I had had the offer and laid down my conditions of acceptance. Well, Ken came up trumps. The Ryder Cup committee not only agreed we should travel first class, they went one better. They booked us on a Concorde to take us to the States, and agreed that our regular caddies could go too! I also decided to do something personally for the team. I felt that it would be nice for all team members to have a memento of the match so I arranged with Waterford Crystal to provide suitably engraved decanters. They wanted to do them for the American side as well, so I contacted Jack Nicklaus. I did not want to wrong-foot him but he was all for the idea, and arranged on his side for both teams to receive glass golf-club heads made by Tiffany. We started a new tradition.

As a matter of fact I nearly resigned as captain several weeks later over a row about the golf bags we were to be issued with. They were plastic and I did not care for them. I wanted Burberry to do them but in the end I had to back down. If we had pulled out of the contract that had been signed for bags, the PGA could have been sued. The problem was that I came in as captain after most of the contracts had been signed. I had to compromise, but that apart, I must say that all the arrangements went exceptionally well. Everyone on the PGA—from Colin Snape who is Executive Director of the Association, based at The Belfry, venue of the 1985 match, and Ken Schofield, the European Tour secretary, right down the line—made sure of that. From a players' point of view it was the best organised yet—spoiled only by the fact that we lost, if only by a point at the end of the day. It will be first class all the way again in 1985.

There was great team spirit in 1983, though I was reported as having said some very unkind and unpleasant things to one member of the side on the way over to Florida. It was said I told Gordon Brand from Yorkshire that because of the rules and regulations of the match, which seemed to get changed every two years, I would play him in the singles but that he could not expect to be played in first-day or second-day foursomes or four-balls. I had decided on my pairings but I honestly do not remember being in any way derogatory about Gordon. If I did say anything which he thought derogatory, I know I would not have meant it to be. Anyway, Gordon only played in the singles and lost to Bob Gilder.

The key man for me at Florida in 1983 was Severiano Ballesteros. He did a marvellous job. I told him that if I did not play him with young Paul Way I could not play Way on the first two days. I told Seve that I felt Paul had considerable talent and that it would rise to the surface if the Spanish star was partnering him. I thought Paul would rise to the occasion inspired by Ballesteros. After the morning play on the second day, Angel Gallardo, the Spanish vice-chairman of the PGA European Tour, came to me telling me Severiano was not very happy. I went into the locker room as he was peeling off his shirt, wet through with perspiration. Seve laid it on the line. He told me he felt like a father to Paul, that he was holding his hand all the way round. I said that was exactly what I had in mind and reminded him that that was why I partnered them. He looked at me. I asked him if there was a problem and he said there was not. The partnership won 2½ points out of 4. Ballesteros' gesture was tremendous.

Ballesteros is a very special man who believes very much in the Cup match now, but you know he very nearly did not play in 1983. He had been so hurt about being left out in 1981 that he refused to commit until well on into the season. I went to him at the Open and caught up with him at breakfast at Birkdale. I sat down with him and said I needed to talk to him about the Cup. He said he did not want to play, but I told him that if he did not everyone would crucify him. I told him it could only do him good if he played, and the team would benefit too. I said I appreciated his problems. I too had been surprised he had been left out in 1981. He surprised me by sympathising with me about my omission. We had a common bond—and not just the pleasant one of having both won the Open. I told him that at first I felt like I wanted to hurt them, that I had been the first to stand up and request that John Jacobs be given a second term as captain and that I had ended up being left out—but that was all in the past. Now we had to work together to win the Cup. It was vital that he play.

His eggs were getting cold. Our chat had lasted half an hour but he agreed to consider his position again. Two weeks later he said he would play. He is a big fellow with a lot of heart, and as a golfer he is getting better and better every year. It was just great getting him on board. Nick Faldo was fantastic for the side too, and Bernard Langer. I never asked anything special of Nick because I knew he would give his all. I've spent a lot of time with him giving him advice from time to time. He listens. He is more of a loner than some on tour but when the chips are down and it is for his country he needs no reminding of the importance of the occasion. As for Langer, he came to me on the second day and asked if he could be dropped as he felt he was not playing well enough. I told him he was a champion because he coped so well and scored so well even when he was not at his best. He went out and in partnership with Faldo took 3 out of 4 points in the four-balls and foursomes. Langer had been on the committee which had vetoed Ballesteros' half-promised participation in 1981, but the two golfers got on well enough. I think Severiano knew that the previous time Langer had been caught up in Ryder Cup politics, trying to play the neutral, but even if he did not fully believe that, no animosity surfaced all week. There was no ill-feeling between them at all; indeed team morale was superb and everyone behaved themselves, especially Ken Brown, quite reformed from 1979.

I had decided before the match started that I would not break up any of my partnerships—the strongest I could field because I knew that to have a chance of winning we needed to be ahead or at the very worst level after two days. Ballesteros and Way did well, and so did Faldo and Langer, but I was disappointed that the Scots Bernard Gallacher and Sandy Lyle did not hit it off. They were not at their best. Lyle had the ball so far out of position at address that I could not believe it. I tried to tell him but it made no difference. He could not correct it in time to find his true form. They were potentially one of my strongest pairings, but you are never going to get a Ryder Cup team in which on the week everyone is playing at his peak. I know that—but I still keep my fingers crossed for every match.

My theory in choosing the partnerships for 1983 was simple enough. I just felt that Langer and Faldo would work well as a team. It was instinct, just as it was with Ballesteros and Way, when I argued to myself that Seve was strong enough to carry the lad who was playing his first Ryder Cup. I knew Ken Brown might be awkward to pair up but that was solved when experienced Brian Waites told me he did not mind playing with Ken. They got on all right, as I knew they would, because Brian, at 44, was a generation older than Ken and quite able to handle him had there been any problems. There were none. I did not want to play Sam and Sandy together. Don't ask me why, because I could not give you a proper answer—I just felt it wouldn't work. They are both instinctive players and if both went wrong at the same time it would have been very problematic, so I put Bernard Gallacher with Sandy, who is so strong when things are going right for him. I argued too that if he needed an odd kick in the pants then Bernard was the boy to give it to him. Unfortunately this pair did not play as well as they can and I could only use them once. I paired Sam with Spaniard Jose Maria Canizares on one occasion, and with the determined Welshman Ian Woosnam in another game. I was invigorated by the challenge of trying to get the pairs right and enjoyed it all very much. It was probably one of the most perfect weeks of my golfing career, marred only by the fact that we lost.

It was a totally different feeling being non-playing captain. When you are playing you have to suppress your feelings. One of the most difficult things about the game of golf, unlike football or rugby or most other games, is that when you feel that rush of adrenalin you have no outlet for it. You can jump around and shout out in the soccer field but you cannot do that on the golf course. In contast, when you feel the adrenalin pumping through your veins you must control it. As the captain of the side I could afford, however, to let the adrenalin out. I could cheer and I did on the course until I was almost hoarse every night. So it was a different kind of pressure for me. Certainly I expended a lot of nervous energy. It was hard work, but what thrills, and the excitement of it all was tremendous.

I went about the course everywhere I felt I was needed. I had two radios, and Tommy Horton and Angel Gallardo kept passing information to me. I was in direct touch with the main scoreboard, and even Lord Derby was funnelling information to me from the games he was watching. The atmosphere was electric.

The drama of the last day had started the previous

afternoon for me, and involved the way I structured the line-up for the singles. I had a fair idea that Jack Nicklaus would put his strength at the bottom, so I opted for strength at the top in the hope of getting points on the board. I also knew I needed an experienced man in the last match. Bernard Gallacher was given that job, and found himself having to try and cope with Tom Watson. The American superstar had been played every day in every series (although he did not want to do so) because Nicklaus considered him an intimidation factor. Watson went along with that, and found himself involved in a tremendous scrap with Bernard, one of the toughest, most determined competitors ever to play for Britain or Europe.

Watson won on the seventeenth to give the Americans the winning point, and Bernard was made to feel by some people as if he had lost the Cup—but that was totally unfair. Someone had to be in the last match, and it is the overall last-day performance by the complete team that decides the issue. Bernard, being such a great competitor, was upset, of course, at losing, but he knew that, had he won, he would have been our biggest hero. He played as well as he could, because he knows no other way, but on the day Watson was just marginally better.

In the Ryder Cup it is all about pride, and nothing to do with money. In fact, although we have been paid in the past, there was no fee last time, nor is there this year. We have opted instead for first class treatment. I speak for all the lads when I say that once every two years we are happy to put money aside and play for the honour and the glory. All we ask is to be treated the same way as the Americans—and we are.

We flew Concorde to America last time; this year the Americans are flying into Birmingham airport on a special Concorde. We can drive to The Belfry, but my team will be kitted out with the best possible clothing—raincoats, cashmere blazers and three golf bags to match the colour scheme of our shirts, slacks and jerseys each day. The idea of three bags incidentally is that each player can keep one of them and give away two to be auctioned for charity.

Our men will be made to feel like kings, and so they

should. They will be facing up to the kind of pressure golfers feel when they are trying to win a major championship and have played themselves into contention. It really was so close last time. At the end of the day I was just disappointed that the boys lost by a slender point. I was sad for them. They had given everything and almost rocked Jack Nicklaus and the Americans back on their heels. All I had done was try to put them together the best way I could to maximise their talents. Once I had decided on my pairings I did not worry about anything and just kept my fingers crossed. All the work was up to the members of the team. I could try to get them in the right frame of mind but they had to do the job. In fact, I did not need to be much of a psychologist because they were all pretty experienced.

I tried to get everything right on the ground. That was of prime importance. Viv and I had a suite attached to our bedroom and I made it known that this was the team's suite, not ours. It was for team use, all week, at any time of the day or night. There would be eats and drinks available throughout the day and in the evening. It was to be our unofficial gathering place and it worked out remarkably well. We shall follow that plan again. From the social point of view the room was vitally important. We wanted it to be somewhere we could relax, and if we did not go to the restaurant it had to be big enough for us to sit and enjoy a steak. Everything was geared to relaxing, with the wives and girlfriends also involved, and everyone mixing—it was great for morale. We had such a good time one night that we signed a cheque for fillet steaks and salads worth $650, but the PGA were happy to pay, and sponsors Bells, the whisky people from Perth, were not complaining either. I was very firm about having the women around. That has not always been allowed but I thought it was essential.

Because it was important to be mentally in the best frame of mind that week I impressed on them all that anything they wanted, within reason, they could and indeed would have. I had no cross words with anyone. Everyone did exactly as they were asked to do and we kept the official functions down to a minimum. The lads were there to play golf and hopefully win, not parade at function after function.

Sometimes these official dates can get in the way of the preparations, and can tense golfers up. Of course as a team we had responsibilities and we did not shirk them, but we refused to go out every night. We did one day go to Jack Nicklaus' home, which was only a few miles away from the course. He and Arnold Palmer, who lived just a mile or so from Latrobe when the Cup match was played there in 1977, must be the only captains of Ryder Cup sides who could enjoy the luxury of staying at home for the match! It was a superb night.

I will not necessarily follow the same pattern of selection this time. For one thing, the composition of the team, while likely to be largely the same, is bound to differ in some respects. I am planning nothing until I see the team and assess how the course will be playing, and what the weather is likely to do, and until I have run the rule over the Americans. All these things must be considered before I decide on tactics. I am excited again about the Cup but I don't dare think about winning. It is my business to get my team in the best possible frame of mind to play their very best and, if they do, then winning will take care of itself. One of the biggest problems for the team members will be coping with the expected massive build-up to the match. So many people on the periphery who do not understand the full implications of the game will believe that because we came so close last time we can easily win at home, but it is not at all like that. Nothing indeed could be further from the truth. There is no question in my mind, however, that I will be leading a team which is capable of winning, and of coping with the pressure put on them by enthusiastic home fans eagerly egging them on.

I don't want the fans to be so enthusiastic that they get carried away and start clapping and cheering if an American misses. I thought the American galleries last time were very impartial and we must be too. Partisan crowds can sometimes be a tremendous boost to the underdogs who feel everyone is against them. I've seen that happen in the World Match-Play. I'll tell my fellows that if the crowds do go over the top a bit then I would like us to diffuse the situation by apologising to the opposition. The more an underdog gets shouted at the more he digs into himself to find the necessary grit, guts and determination to win, and if the Americans find themselves in the unusual role of underdogs you can bet they will not be slow to switch that to their advantage by trying even harder to beat us. It could be hurtful to us if our followers are too partisan, and if the enthusiasm which inevitably there will be becomes too one sided and embarrassing my boys will even ask our fans—in the nicest possible way—to 'ease off'.

I believe we will have our best shot at winning this year because we should have a particularly strong side of international players, most of whom will have played before in the fixture. We no longer have an inferiority complex because our fellows know they are as good as the bulk of the Americans—in fact last time Jack Nicklaus made the point that we drove the ball further and straighter than the average Americans. What we need to be is razor sharp around and on the greens. This time the American side is being chosen from the current money list, which means there could be a number of new boys in the side. No matter how experienced the newcomers are, how confident and controlled, they will feel the pressure a great deal. Americans do not get many chances to represent their country and I am just banking on the game being played in a rough squally week at The Belfry.

As for the venue, well I have always believed the match should be played on a seaside course when it is held in this country. Politics should take second place when it comes to venue choice. I think the more compromising the Americans have to do, the better chance we have. Our European players are far more used to having to adjust their game to cope with American conditions than the US players are to adjusting to British seaside golf. When we don't play the match at the seaside, then some of our advantage is immediately lost, in my opinion. I realise the reasons for the venue for 1985, and am happy with it but urge a seaside venue to be considered in future!

I have felt for some time that in Ryder Cup years we should do a deal with the Royal and Ancient Golf Club at St Andrews and the club hosting the Open, which is always played on a links. If we could retain the stands or at least some of them we could play the Cup match at the Open venue and avoid a great deal of expense and trouble, and gain what could be the upper hand when it blows. I know how well the Americans do in the Open on links courses but it is never as rough in July as it can be in September or October at the seaside—remember the tournaments that were staged for several years at Turnberry when we were all nearly blown away during the autumn equinox. In one John Player Classic, Johnny Miller just gave up because he could not stand up in the wind! Anyway if it is inland this time we will just need to go out and win—for the first time since 1957 when the venue was Lindrick—on another course a long way from the sea. Maybe that is an omen, and I shall be trying to set up The Belfry to suit the games of our players this time.

It is difficult for me to assess how to do that in a way that could give our players any slight advantage over the US team headed by Lee Trevino. The more difficult I make the pin placements the more I'll be pandering to the Americans, who are used to playing target golf to tough positions all year in the States. The Americans are lavish and genuinely generous hosts, but not when it comes to setting up their courses for the match on Stateside. I've often felt our hierarchy do not realise how crafty the Americans are. For instance, they know that we are not used in Britain to playing on fast greens, so they would cut the greens three times a day at The Greenbrier—morning, lunchtime and evening—to make sure they were the glassiest they could possibly be because that suited their players more than ours. We never seem to take that kind of advantage. We are far too sportsmanlike in that respect. Indeed, I am sure some of our officials did not even realise what the Americans were doing to the course at the Greenbrier.

We must realise that when we are the hosts we have the advantage of choosing not only the venue but also the way to set the course up. The Americans are smart enough to have realised that and to fix the courses to suit their players with a smile and a friendly nod. It is time we took full advantage in this country, so I'll have my own ideas about how The Belfry should be played. There is little point in having thicker rough than normal because, although we will in general be longer hitters than they are, we are no straighter than them and could find ourselves in as much trouble if not more than them if the rough was grown extra long. I'll talk to a few of my team, assess their various strengths and weaknesses in respect of their games and then plan accordingly. I just hope it blows like hell—like it does at the seaside. I believe that I will want to play the course as long as possible using the very back tees at the par-3s to give my men the chance of getting up and making it difficult for some of the Americans. That would be a blatant move. There are other, subtler ways I can help my team—but it would be foolish to give away the secrets. To win the match we need to do well on the first-and second-day four-balls and foursomes. We need a good start to increase confidence throughout the side.

It would be nice to end my competitive career with a win at The Belfry. Being captain came at a nice time in my career. It is not an easy job but I would never take anything away from the players. The players win the Ryder Cup not the captain, whose job is just to get them in the best possible frame of mind for the job in hand.

It's no secret that when it was all over two years ago, Jack Nicklaus, delighted to have won—just as I would have been—drew me aside and said he felt a draw would have been a fairer result. I would have been happy with a draw but nothing is ever totally fair in golf.

In the end, the difference between winning and losing is simply a question of taking, no, grabbing your opportunities—sometimes once-in-a-lifetime opportunities. The winners are the takers in golf, nice guys maybe, but the golfers who, when the chips are down, are the hard men. We came awfully close last time, and this year the conditions are totally different but it should be a great contest, and if we do our best we can win. European golf has never been so strong in depth as it is now. We are ready.

18
Fun and Games

Up until now I have had everything I want out of life, but I'm a realist and I appreciate that getting the most out of life does not mean being happy all the time. Life is a compromise, balancing achievement with contentment. It demands patience and understanding. What is happiness after all? I am happy about a lot of things—my family's health, for instance—but that does not mean I am happy with everything. There is no such thing as perfect happiness, just as there is no perfect peace or perfect anything. As things have gone so far, I am very happy because I have a great family and a great wife. I am involved in and around the game that on the whole has been good to me. I am well occupied with plenty to do. I am making money. I still have challenges I want to win. I am always striving to make things better for us as a family, and then the next process will be to look at my children and help them to get on. More and more now my interests will move towards them.

Fortunately I am well off financially. I remember Gary Player saying to me ten years ago that he could not work out in real money terms what was 'enough'. At the time I suggested to him that half a million pounds in the bank would surely see him right—in those days that was over a million dollars. I don't think that any more. It's all relative anyway. Enough is never enough in terms of finance. Everything's going up all the time, to the extent that I assess it all this way: to me now £10 million is a lot of money, £5 million all right and a million is just sort of OK. Does that sound pretentious? It's what I feel.

Because I am still earning from that Open win it is tough to put a figure on what Lytham's triumph was worth to me. The fact that I am still doing lucrative company days today is

198

a result of having been Open champion. I know I grabbed at everything I could in the early days, but that was because of basic insecurity about money. Financially I always think I am going to go broke—I am terribly insecure about money and always have been. I know I am used to the good life and thought I had it cracked a year or so back, but look at what has happened in the financial markets around the world. I am no longer as 'flush' as I thought I was, so I am always looking around for a new deal. I no longer know what is enough to maintain my living standards and ensure a firm financial foundation for the kids. When we left the house in Jersey it was costing us £30,000 a year to run but expenses have been rising all the time as the kids get older.

I used to think the family and I had no more money worries for life because we had invested the money I made wisely, but I am not so sure about things now. It is still wisely invested but is it going to be enough to help us all cope in a crisis? Of course I would have the option, if times got really bad, of cutting back on my lifestyle without having to live a life of misery, and we could live in a much smaller house—but I hope it never comes to that. I've got what I've got by hard work. I'd hate it all to disappear through no real fault of my own!

Personally I would not mind having a million pounds in the bank giving me interest at 10 per cent and assuring me of £100,000 pounds a year. I would know if I stayed inside that budget I was OK! Of course it is not as simple as that. I have plots of land here and an apartment, and it is so difficult to tie all the financial ends up tidily to give me the feeling of total security. I always feel as if I have to go out and work harder and harder to make more and more. It is in my nature. But almost as important to me as wealth and position is my image. It is always important to have a sound image publicly—and I think I have.

My income has been around £100,000-£200,000 a year for the past ten years. My worst year was 1981 when I made £80,000 and spent £81,000. I did not play so many tournaments that year and because of that my income was lower, but I'm not nearly as interested in the money I have made in the past as in what I hope to make in the future down in Spain. Recently I have been earning £60,000-£70,000 a year on the course and another £40,000-£50,000 off it with contracts of one kind and another. Sometimes I have spent £60,000 to make that. I was spending £40,000 on manager's fees—McCormack took a percentage of the prize money I earned as well as a slice of the contract money. Then there were caddy fees, hotels, travel and all the rest. The bottom line is that now I am far more interested in my new lifestyle, in which I will effectively trim the travelling expenses to a minimum and yet be involved in business ventures related to golf which will pull in more than I was earning as a regular player.

Most of the long-term contracts I signed were for four or five years but as you get older you do not tend to sign such long-term deals. I know Henry Cotton has contracts which have run into his '70s, and it is nice to get a longer-term one when you get on a bit, but companies are far more strict these days than they used to be. Money is not thrown about the way it has been in the past.

Compared with those people who do not even have a job — over 3 million in Britain alone—I have no worries at all. Many people retired in the '60s with £250,000 and thought that was a vast amount, and it was in the '60s. It no longer is.

I don't like taking chances with money, which may be a throwback to my father. I don't know a lot about the Stock Exchange although I am a Lloyd's underwriter operating with eleven syndicates. I have a good spread of money. Being an underwriter means I have to show I can easily liquidate £100,000 at short notice and that effectively means having £200,000 in collateral to cover that. I've taken out insurance policies against being hit with heavy claims but I've been happy so far making a small profit each year on my investment. If somebody came up to me and said they knew where I could make 50 per cent on my money then I would know there has to be a massive risk and only a slightly smaller risk at 25 per cent or 20 per cent profit. I'm not in the risk business. I've worked too hard too long to get what I've got to jeopardise anything. If I can get 10 per cent on my money and keep adding to the capital each year then I'm very satisfied.

McCormack's Organisation continues to look after all my financial affairs. I might take £5,000 and put it into something they recommend will do well, and generally speaking what they have recommended has done well, but I'm careful with cash. The bulk of my money, like the Lloyd's underwriting business, is in Jersey, making me 10 per cent at the end of each year after tax. I have the Lloyd's money on top of that—and that might earn me anything from £10,000 to £18,000 a year just for showing the money up front. I am happy to let money grow slowly.

I have met plenty of fly men in my time and just don't want to know about any harebrained schemes. I am always looking for consistent returns to meet my expanding demand, and so far everything is all right. My diary is always well filled with company engagements which are financially worthwhile; there will be the prize money from the few events I choose to play and there will be my television cheques. At the end of the year it should all turn out fine, but I plan to hold on to more than I did in the early '70s, when I spent almost as quickly as I earned. In those days under the Wilson government, I was paying 83 per cent tax—83p to the government in every £1 I earned. I was staying in suites at hotels and buying big cars just to thwart the tax man. If I didn't spend it he would take it. If I had stayed in Britain instead of moving to Jersey and then on to Spain I would have been broke by now. Having earned all the money I have, I would still, I am sure, be broke. It's amazing but that is the way the tax system works in Britain. That is why I had to leave and that is why other top sportsmen will have to leave eventually too. Regardless of how much they are making now it will become necessary, I think, for them to operate from an overseas base. That is if they want to get as much out of their game as I have got out of mine.

When we were in Jersey it was easy to keep tabs on expenditure by using the monthly information forwarded by McCormack from the various credit card organisations—I could detail things down to a penny. It is different in Spain where so much is on a cash-down basis. It is much tougher to keep tabs on things! I've not been involved in the cash business in years but everything is OK as long as I don't overspend. We want for nothing, however, and that is the way I'd like it to be for the rest of my life. Who wouldn't?

I get a big kick out of doing a good deal—I mean a deal in which everyone wins. I make a few bob, the customer is satisfied, and everybody is happy. If I do a company day, for instance, I get well paid for it and if it goes well then I have a good feeling inside. I like doing a good job as much as I enjoy making money. I was in a London cab recently and the chap was one of those talkative types. He told me he had the Beatle Paul McCartney in his taxi the week before. He had asked him what was 'in it' these days for McCartney, what with all his money and all that. McCartney replied that he just enjoyed making money—that simple—because he still has, lurking somewhere under the surface, a feeling of insecurity, and that is me to a tee too—only more so, because I am worth only a fraction of what Paul McCartney is worth.

In a way my insecurity, well controlled but nevertheless always there, just serves to keep me ever eager to meet new people and make new, bigger, more lucrative deals. I don't do anything big for nothing, but I don't always do things for ready cash. I do get involved in contra-deals when, for example, a client may provide a car for me in England for services I provide. This is the modern style—so different from what I used to get involved in. Some deals have taken me to unusual spots.

I once played at Dubbo in the Australian outback about an hour and a half's plane ride on an old Viscount from Sydney. I played an exhibition match there and it was terrible. There were more flies there than I would have ever thought possible. Flies got up your nose, in your ears— everywhere. It was in the middle of nowhere, out in kangaroo country where the Australians spoke with an even broader accent than normal. I never saw any kangaroos on the course, but I have taken care to look out for leopards when I've played in Africa. At Karen, that lovely club on the outskirts of Nairobi, they have a sign to warn you not to hang around if one comes padding out of the bush. That's an occasion when you can legitimately leave the course without penalty. In Thailand, at the Siam Country Club, they have another problem—armed bandits who use a path across the course as a short-cut from their camps to Bangkok. They leave the golfers alone as long as no one tries to tangle with them!

It is much safer playing golf in the country-club atmosphere of America although not every course is as plush as Seminole or Muirfield Village, Jack's multi-million dollar course in Ohio where the Ryder Cup will be played in 1987. I once flew to one of those small regional airports in the Mid West with Vivien and was picked up by a fellow in a station wagon to be driven through the night for an hour and a half to our destination. It was 1 o'clock when we arrived and we frankly wondered whether we had come to the right place. The clubhouse was a tiny wooden cottage-type building and it was obvious the steward of the club, our driver, had moved out with his wife to let Viv and I have the one bedroom. He settled us in then disappeared—heaven knows where, because the place seemed so remote.

When we woke up in the morning and looked out of the hut there was a green outside as big as a large-sized dinner table—20 sq ft—and next to it a hole, just a hole, to act as a bunker. It was only nine holes and it was in the worst condition you could ever imagine. Apparently they had had Doug Sanders there the year before and it had been a great success, hence my being booked in for an eighteen-hole exhibition match with some locals. The chap who owned the club was on some sort of ego trip, I am sure, coming up with $4,000 to get Sanders and then me there. 'It's some place, isn't it?' he said with a smile as we climbed into the station wagon to return to the airport. It sure was and I know I could never find it again. Indeed as the years have rolled on I have to pinch myself to make sure that it really happened! The people were really nice but it was one of those occasions when you think 'What the hell am I doing here?'—like you say when you have been caught overnight in New York and find yourself in an airport hotel with a room about as big as a cupboard. You put the key in the door, open up and you nearly break the window, it is so small. There is a television in the corner, a bed and a chair and you think—is this really the glamour of golf? You have nine hours to kill and when you have triple-locked the door to try to avoid being robbed you fall into a fitful sleep. Now that I don't miss . . .

I never read as a child but I read now—popular novels by Irwin Shaw, Frederick Forsyth, Jack Higgins. It was the golf tour that started me reading books, just to pass the time in places like that airport hotel. I've packed some reading into the last 20 years but it has all been light stuff. I'm no Bernard Gallacher, who reads political histories and autobiographies of the world's statesmen! That's serious work!

Indeed, the whole tour is a much more serious business than it used to be. We seemed to have more laughs in the old days. I suppose the funniest thing I ever saw was when Tommy Horton and I were playing in Africa behind Lionel Platts and Fred Boobyer in the '60s. Lionel went up to his caddy on the green and told him to attend the flag. Platts was looking down at the grass trying to see which way the grain ran—in fact it was growing in all directions—as he walked back to his marker. Meanwhile the young caddy, misunderstanding the instruction, had removed the flag and was standing strictly to attention some five yards to the right of where the hole was. When he got back to his marker Platts replaced the ball, looked up and saw the caddy standing to attention with the flag. Then he hit the putt so perfectly that he shouted to the caddy 'Take the pin out, for God's sake, take the pin out.' The caddy stood transfixed as if he was looking at a man with two heads, because the hole, after all, was five yards away. The pin was out! Lionel was not happy because, needless to say, after all that kerfuffle he missed the next putt as well. There is an advantage to having your own caddy with you every week—although long-term relationships have caused problems.

I have not had many caddies. I've had Willie Hilton who carried for me from 1967 to 1973, including my Open victory. He was with me in the really important years. Willie was a good caddy, and I had an excellent relationship with him. I was just looking for someone to carry the bag, and encourage me when I needed to be encouraged, and who knew the job, knew the game. Willie fitted the bill perfectly. He came from Glasgow and had played a bit himself. If I was in doubt about clubbing Willie would just add his pennyworth. We would discuss the shot. He sometimes gave me the confidence I needed but at the end of the day we ran into difficulties—we got too close—and parted company. I don't know what went wrong really—I maybe started paying him too much. I was paying him a lot of money and in the winter of 1973 he asked for another £200 to help him move house, but he failed to move; I was annoyed and we split up. It was a shame because he had been getting top money—£4,000 a year including all his bonuses. Then there was 'Creamy' in the States—Creamy Caralone, who used to shag balls with a baseball glove. I used him in America, and for a time I used Chris Alvarez who seemed like a nice young chap. He caddied for me at the start of 1969 before I came back to win the Open but when I returned to America to continue my US Tour programme, he was not around. He had murdered a chap and ended up in jail. I could hardly believe it. He was inside for seven years and kept writing me letters from prison about how he had made a terrible mistake and how he would like to pick up where he left off when he came out of the penitentiary. I did not think that was such a good idea. Curiously we were not allowed to use our own caddies at the US Open in 1970, and a young fellow, a student, worked for me then.

Back in Britain, with the departure of Willie Hilton, I used a member of my house staff, Phil Rumble, as my caddy. Phil did not know a thing about golf. He was the son of one of my gardeners at Gloucester where we were staying at that time. I had to find something for him to do. He was a chauffeur, valet, handyman, a do-everything Man-Friday type whom I tried to train up. I had to teach him everything—how to carry the bag, where to stand as I was playing round, when to take the pin out and when not to. I taught him from nothing, but there was this other fellow at the house who used to put a couple of fire bricks in the bottom of the bag just to make it even heavier. I'm not so sure Phil ever rumbled that. I got golf shoes for him and in 1973 I won the Dunlop Masters with him. We never spoke as we played round. I gave orders but he remained silent all the time, no doubt petrified that he would step out of line and get me disqualified. It wouldn't have mattered if he had spoken because he was a right cockney and I could not understand half of what he was saying anyway. He used to drink eight gallons of beer a week, eight pints a night and sixteen pints on Sunday— except those Sundays he was caddying for me when he dispensed with his eight at lunchtime. And he looked like a beanpole.

It was when Phil was with us that we had a very stuck-up nanny working for us. When I sacked her in the Far East, it was Phil I telephoned, asking him to pick her up at the airport and drop her at a station somewhere. He not only picked her up, he married her!

Phil went when we left Gloucester and I then employed until 1981 another Scot, Scotty Gilmour, who was a joiner by trade. He used to walk a lot with me in America after he had finished caddying for Chi Chi Rodriguez. I liked Scotty, but like all caddies he was a roamer and eventually he decided to move on as well. He had helped around the house on Jersey and I had offered him a full-time job when he was not caddying but he did not want to stay—it would tie him down too much. Maybe, like Willie Hilton, he and I got too close. I used to take him out for meals and certainly enjoyed his company but latterly he was not doing his job properly.

Someone had started to sell yardage books of the courses we played and Scotty started buying them and not pacing the course as he was expected to do for me. We had a bit of a row and split up, and I decided I would never again have a permanent caddy. Scotty always had the wanderlust and headed back to the States, but he is usually around here in the summer. I'm sure he will be doing well. He is a survivor who can take the knocks. He once put all his savings on a horse that cleared the last fence lengths in front, and at a good price, only to fall on the run in! After Scotty, Geoff Pymar, the former speedway star, used to carry the bag from time to time, or one of the kids pulled it on a trolley. Geoff, at 73, was super-fit and as wealthy as I was, so it would have been an insult to offer him a wage, but I gave him sweaters, got him invited to parties, luncheons, all sorts of occasions, and he loved being involved. He enjoyed rubbing shoulders with top players like Seve, Nicklaus and Watson. Geoff was an avid golfer himself and just wanted to be part of the scene, but I understand he went off and got married to a Thailander. He fell for her on a visit to Bangkok and she wanted to come to England. The only way that was possible was for him to marry her, so he did, but I've temporarily lost contact with him. Geoff used to live on raisins and nuts. He was a real health fanatic! He practised his own golf very hard but with no regard for the method he was using, which was not a good one. He had a built-in loop in his swing.

Looking back, I did enjoy the relationship I had with Willie and Scotty. There are no hard feelings between us, no animosity at all. We had good times and we all enjoyed ourselves. At the 1969 Open Willie was very helpful. I was jabbering away to him going down the third and fourth holes and I said I just had to talk. He nodded and kept very calm. That calmness helped me! We had a load of laughs.

I used to have a great sense of humour on tour. I knew all the latest gags, all the funniest jokes. Trevino used to know them too and we would have quite a session in the locker rooms. As for the lads today, Langer has little or no sense of humour, Sandy Lyle has, and Nick Faldo doesn't mind a joke, but everyone is so much more earnest with so much money at stake—much more so than when I was playing really well years ago. David Jagger from Yorkshire used to be a prankster on tour then and he fooled so many people so often that it was incredible. Once in Italy he convinced a large number of his colleagues that a special bus would arrive at 2 am to take them to Milan airport to catch an Air India flight to London in order to beat an Alitalia strike scheduled to begin at 9 o'clock the next morning, a strike that would prevent many of them getting home. They all packed and were downstairs for the bus in the middle of the night— except Jagger who was fast asleep! Of course it was one of Jagger's pranks. Some of the older fellows were less than amused by that one. We laugh about that kind of thing more now than we did at the time!

At the Lawrence Batley tournament held at Bingley St

Ives one year I was standing on the tee at the seventeenth with Ken Brown. There was a hold-up and two fans were taking pictures. I noticed one nudge the other and say 'Go on take Jacko . . ', but his friend indicated that he had me. 'Quick, take Ken Brown then' was the retort, to which the other fellow answered sharply, 'Why, there's no rush. He plays so slow I could do an oil painting of him.' Ken did not hear but I told him later. He just smiled.

19
The New Young Breed

Severiano Ballesteros is the best player Europe has ever produced. I was never as good as the dark-haired Spaniard, who has won twice as many majors as I did and who is still only 28. He has won thirty events around the world, which speaks volumes for his talent. Like Gary Player he can win anywhere. I was good but he has a different lifestyle, which has helped him and his golf in the last five years. He has none of the family obligations which I had to worry him and get in the way of winning, but that apart I still think he is the best striker we have ever had in Europe. I would put Bernhard Langer a close second to Seve as far as striking the ball is concerned, especially those long irons. He beat the yips too, which took courage, and went on to win the US Masters. He is one of the most dedicated golfers I have ever come up against. Like Seve he knows what he wants, and like Seve he will get it. He is a one-man golfing country really, because no one else in Germany matches up to him in international status, which sometimes means that the Germans cannot field a decent team—and sometimes cannot provide a team at all.

Then there is Sandy Lyle, that marvellously likeable lump of a lad, one of the best strikers of a golf ball there is, although I'm not too sure he really knows what makes it all happen. It is as if he is playing by feel and instinct, and when it goes wrong he cannot work it out quickly enough. He'll be tremendous when he breaks that barrier. Right now he will win two or three times a year anyway, but he needs a push. He has no idea how good he is. I hesitate to think how good he would be if he had Gary Player's attitude – but then God never gave any golfer everything. It is all so automatic with him, but then he has been playing since he was three—and his young son Stuart I reckon will beat dad to the tee in age.

He toddles around all day at some events, learning early about the Tour his father could dominate later in his career, when others have perhaps burned themselves out to a degree. Sandy was bold enough just over a year ago to change his grip to interlocking, with tremendous results, although he later went back to overlapping. Whichever grip he uses, however, on form he is awesome off the tee. With a 1-iron he hits further than most people using a driver. And just for variation he will switch round and hit left-handed if you want. Golf is in his blood, with his father a pro and his late uncle too. Even his wife Chrissie was a pro on the expanding women's Tour before opting out to travel the world with Sandy and young Stuart. He hits the ball further without effort than anyone I know. He benefits from the combination of a very long body, very strong legs and incredibly fast hands, generating, or helping the legs to generate, tremendous firepower.

I have to put Faldo ahead of Lyle, however, because he manages his game so much better. He only started playing when he was thirteen—ten years after Sandy—so is much more mechanical in technique, even if there is a superb flowing action with the swing. He worked hard, taking full advantage of the conditions in America, to tighten up what had been far too loose a swing, and now he is most impressive. He has a less warm personality than Lyle, and is more of a loner, and they have not always got on—but each respects the other's qualities, and it is great to have two such talented international stars as these insisting they do not want to turn their backs on the circuit where they learned the game. To be truthful, while it is necessary to play extensively in America to get the experience to compete at the top level internationally, it is now much more easy to play golf internationally from Britain, once you have reached top grade. Our golfers charge around the world in more comfort than I used to, gaining masses of experience more quickly and stuffing all kinds of currencies in their pockets. Faldo has raised his game in the past at the Open—the hardest of all the majors for a British player to win. There is far less pressure on a British player at the Masters, for instance, but Faldo has not been able to get the emotional charge he gets in the Open when he tees up at Augusta. It is a pity. If he does, one year he could win a Green Jacket.

Another have-clubs-will-travel golfer is Sam Torrance from Largs in Scotland, who is, like Sandy, the son of a pro. He has terrific talent too, even if I have always felt he had far too strong a grip—a grip I am surprised neither he nor his father Bob has thought to change. He has a great eye for a ball and can really crunch the drives if he has half a mind to. He had a great year in 1984, winning as much as would have earned him No. 1 spot most years, only he ran into Langer on a four-wins season, and more especially played with him to see the West German score a brilliant 62 round the El Saler course at Valencia, which clinched the money-table top spot. It was cruel that he had to watch from close range as Langer turned on his best performance of the season outside the Open, where he tied second, of course, with Watson, behind Ballesteros.

Curiously, like Torrance, I have always felt that Langer and Yorkshireman Howard Clark have grips that are too strong as well. With too strong a left hand I've noticed their bad shots are snap hooks. This makes it harder work for them under pressure than it would be if they had a more neutral grip like Hogan forced himself to use. Mind you, Langer did not make many mistakes last spring when he won the Masters and the Sea Pines Heritage Classic, on a very tight course, the following week. Changing your grip is never easy but maybe he has moved his hands into a more neutral position on the club now.

Of all the top golfers in Britain and Europe, the best putter for consistency is Faldo —I don't know how he does it. It is Ballesteros for flair, and Torrance for tempo. It never changes—and Langer, after all the work he has put into putting, is as deadly on long putts as Bob Charles, the left-hander from New Zealand.

European golf is remarkably buoyant at the moment. I have not mentioned another man with a magic putting touch—low-scoring Jose Maria Canizares of Spain, who with Jose Rivero won the World Cup in Rome last year. Manuel Pinero is another Spaniard with masses of guts for his size, and back in Britain there are Howard Clark and Ken Brown. Howard would have preferred, I think, to have changed to a more consistent swing if he could, but found it too difficult to change his grip, and as for Ken—what a worker he is. He is improving his swing all the time, but the fact is that he has had to work hard because of the swing. In the past he has had a tendency for him to speed up and flail at the ball with the club head. He has the problem which Peter Oosterhuis also faces of being extra tall. The ideal height for a golfer is about 5ft 10in and the ideal weight about 11 stone—and would you believe it, I filled the bill exactly (in the old days I would hasten to add).

I am encouraged by the talent around—talent like that of pint-sized Ian Woosnam, who on his day can outputt anyone, even Bernard Gallacher, as he did to win the Silk Cut Masters two years ago at St Pierre, that always beautifully manicured course down by Chepstow. He has to be able to putt well because he is a little wayward off the tee as he tries to generate extra hitting power to compensate for his small build—just 5ft 4in. Ronan Rafferty, on the other hand, from Northern Ireland—the young man who broke so many Irish and British amateur records—is learning fast—and watch out for great things from Philip Parkin.

All in all, it has been a long time since we could provide such strength in depth for the Ryder Cup, which I hope augurs well for The Belfry. Our lads, once hampered by having a massive inferiority complex in front of the Americans, have shed that particular albatross from their golfing necks. Now, with heads held as high as and as proud as peacocks, they are no longer frightened. Worldwide success has effectively got rid of that second-class citizen status, and that's great.

The European Tour is loaded with talent—but it is a tour plagued somewhat by golfing slowcoaches—some of them talented! I cannot abide a time-waster. That is why Ken Brown used to annoy me. It was not because he was a slow player—he was simply a time-waster. It would be his turn to hit but he would not have put on his golf glove and would take a full 15 seconds to do so while his partners hung around and waited. He could have put the glove on as he walked from the previous green. And when he did eventually tee the ball up it would not be the right height, and he would spend time, wasting our time if not his, adjusting it. I could put the ball in the ground correctly every time without thinking. Australian Noel Ratcliffe is another one who wastes time. He invariably arrives on the tee without any tees in his pocket. As his partners tee up he is rummaging about in his bag to try and find a tee, and if he is first off, everyone is delayed. It's ridiculous.

Maybe a couple of years ago if the authorities had been stricter with Ken Brown they could have cured him once and for all, but they worry about players bringing law suits, claiming their earning ability is being affected—and it would be if they slapped penalty shots on them for their time-wasting, but it would be their own fault. How could they sue anyway? If you are late on the tee you are disqualified and earn no money at all and there are no exceptions to this rule, and no one sues if they fall victim to it—it was no good Seve trying to sue the USGA when he was late on the tee at the US Open. There needs to be closer supervision of time-wasters by the field staff; then those who are consistently slow could be docked two shots. I guarantee that would speed up the slowcoaches. Sometimes I wonder about our officials and the way they handle those situations, but I don't care enough any more to want to change it. I could have, and would have, had I wanted to, but I knew how much resistance there would be to changing the system. Changing it would have benefited the Tour and gained even greater respect for the men running the Tour, but the majority of the guys I would have been doing it for, my fellow players, would not have appreciated it.

Many of them just show up to play. They just come out of the woodwork to play for whatever a sponsor cares to put up. They are not interested in anything other than the money. I am interested in the money too, but I was also interested in getting a great circuit operating as efficiently as possible. Ken Schofield, the executive director who took over from John Jacobs, is doing a great job keeping the money going up and up, but many of the players frankly don't appreciate what he is doing for them. I began to feel I was wasting my time working on their behalf. So now I'm looking after myself and my own career. I'm no longer on the committee. On the face of it that might sound selfish, and it is. Yet if I do a good job on television or entertain customers well down at Sotogrande, or play well somewhere and give those people watching me pleasure, then golf is benefiting as well as me. I am putting my ideas and thoughts into the game as well as earning myself.

Jack Nicklaus is putting back a great deal into golf, building all those magnificent golf courses around the world, but at the same time he is making money, lots of money, for himself, which is great. That way, everybody wins. He is so respected that the authorities in the States listen carefully to what he has to say and act quickly if necessary to put his proposals into practice. Here in Europe I sometimes wonder if we want to be organised or not. Certainly the European Tour is far better organised today than it has ever been but we are not as well organised yet as the Americans were fifteen years ago. We don't have the money the American Tour has, but sometimes we may be too ready just to let things roll along. We have gone all exempt, of course, and are at last doing something positive about slow play. I do believe there are enough caring people around to ensure continued improvement. The caring people are the ones who ring the changes.

20
Now For the Future

People have always felt I was lucky. I have been sometimes—haven't we all?—but we make our own luck. I mean if everything goes well down in Spain, people may again say that I've been lucky, but that's rubbish. I made this situation myself. It's nothing to do with luck that I'm just a few miles from Gibraltar, whose border with Spain was opened earlier this year. Way back in 1976 I said to the McCormack people that when I quit playing in America full time I wanted a place to base myself in Europe—I wanted the sun on my back in winter. They got me a deal at Sotogrande. There was no money in it for me at the start because they did not have any money to give me here, but I earned a fifth of an apartment up at Las Aves—as the new course used to be called—for each of five years. That set up a link with the area and I learned to like it. Indeed I loved it, and saw a future there, and from then on everything that has happened has been up to me. It was my decision to try and make it a more permanent base. So it would be easy for people to say I have been lucky, but I have not really—it was all carefully planned. I am, after all, a doer—I'm not the kind of fellow who sits on his backside and just talks about doing things.

I put all the plusses down on one side of the paper and the minuses on the other, and the former easily outnumber the latter. There's the sun for one thing—all day—and I do like that. Then the courses are so good, right up and down the Costa del Sol, and more are planned for completion before the turn of the century. Communications with Britain, and the rest of the world, are improving all the time. The latest advance will shortly enable us to get English television stations by satellite. I've been known to be impetuous in the past, and made one whopper of a blunder with that mansion down in Gloucester, but this move to Spain is a carefully considered thing. I am not as impetuous as I used to be in anything these days, although I must admit that if I were to see a good opportunity to make money I'd relish the challenge.

I am always looking for outlets for my talent, and in the case of the Spanish connection I am capitalising on my name in the long-term way I always wanted the McCormack Organisation to arrange. I am building my own course and I see no reason why it should be other than a huge success now that the border with Gibraltar is open and there is a major airport 20 minutes away. The area is slap bang in the middle of a development area. I think it will all work out especially the exciting plan to open my own country club just a few miles away from Sotogrande. I have spent time in America learning how to run a country club, and so many people have been very helpful.

I want to be where the opportunities are and that for me is Spain not England, where the weather is so bad and in winter golf courses are unplayable, under snow, flooded, bone hard. I shall continue playing on my own terms as long as I feel like it. If I decide in a year or two that five tournaments a year is not too many then I shall play five. I frankly cannot envisage a situation, even in five years time, when I will not be playing at all, but whatever I am doing—playing or not playing—it will not make a vast difference to the way I will be running my life. Any competitive golf I am involved in will not disrupt the family schedule the way it used to. I'm slowing down a bit—and that is not a bad thing. All my life I've been hyperactive, unable to sit very long in one place, always looking for something different to do almost before I have finished doing what I am doing at the moment. Now I actually do sit down and watch a video or take time to plan my life properly. And the plan for the next four years involves total diversification into golf-related spheres—my new country club project, house development, and organising the rental and sometimes sale of golf carts.

Basically what happened with the carts was that when

216

we arrived in Sotogrande the company operating the complex said to me that I could, if I wanted, have the golf-cart concession. It seemed attractive because I was having to rent the shop and it seemed a way of offsetting some of those costs. There was only one big snag—there were no carts available for rent at the club. If I wanted to do it I would have to import them. I decided, however, that it made good business sense to get involved, and initially imported eight carts. They are Japanese, petrol driven, but assembled in Britain. Petrol-driven carts, I knew from experience, are far more efficient to run than electric ones that need to be recharged every night and which can run out of juice, in my experience, around the sixteenth! There was no chance of our carts doing that. We still have to pay 60 per cent tax on them, but they have proved so popular with the older golfers down here that we have now brought in 60 of them. Some I have sold on a private basis—they cost £5,000 retail—but the others are on a rental basis at courses up and down the Costa del Sol.

I make a 20 per cent profit on sales. For rental, we charge a fee of £20 a round. We give 20 per cent of all rental revenue to the club where the carts are based, and from the rest we take our profit and keep the carts serviced and ensure the tanks are always full at the beginning of the day. The £20 might seem expensive to a British golfer but it is not as far as the Americans are concerned, and we are getting more and more of them holidaying in southern Spain. The fee is equivalent to the cost of hiring two caddies (£8, plus a £2 tip each) and everyone seems happy enough. I know we are. I learned a long time ago that there is nothing you can do about the cost of things and the difficulty of paying for them except to make enough money to do so. It is no good sitting on your backside and complaining about prices. You have to go out and hustle to make more so you can still afford the things you want. If you are not prepared to do that then you have no cause to complain about the expense of living. That's the way I see it—albeit from a reasonably privileged position. I left England because the tax laws cut down my earning capacity. I left Jersey because

I could not adequately expand my earning capacity, and I am now in Spain expecting substantially to improve my financial situation. It's that simple.

The most important aspect of forming the new businesses down here in Spain is getting the people right, getting the property we are selling right, and having an efficient office service and back-up operation. The legal side must be watertight, of course, so that the foundations on which we are building our business are secure and firm.

We borrowed £100,000 to start the cart project off and we shall pay that off in a year. The business is definitely there but we had to go out and get it. I went up and down the coast knocking on doors and signing the deals. There is not a lot of money in the construction business just yet but I had to bring £50,000 into Spain to stock the shop at Sotogrande. I got the best staff, including Derek Brown as manager. He was trained at Gleneagles by Ian Marchbank, and in my opinion is the best in the business. I needed someone in the shop I could trust, someone with loads of experience. Whatever I pay Derek, he is worth every penny, but more importantly he is a good and loyal friend. He will join me in my new club.

I am lucky too in that I enjoy doing the kind of things I am getting involved in now. I enjoy the thrill of business, and was not interested at all in designing golf courses like so many of my colleagues do when they stop playing golf full time. I dabbled in it, of course, and will work hard on designing my own course at my own place in the sun. I could not be happier, because I am a home bird.

I like log fires and barbeques and anything about my home and its surroundings. I am supposed to be a true Cancerian even if I do think that astrology is a load of nonsense. Home is where I want to be, after having been so long on the road, for so long on show. Now I adore going through my front door and just disappearing from the world. I'm no recluse but it is nice to have somewhere to hide.

I am learning Spanish gradually but I am not taking lessons any more. I found it all too taxing. I cannot sit down after 25 years and start being taught again as if I was at school. I learn more from just listening to my Spanish friends. I am sure that in three years I will be able to speak reasonable Spanish. One of the reasons I can afford to be lazy is that so many people in Southern Spain speak English anyway, and the numbers will increase following the opening of the border with Gibraltar earlier this year. I am a person who makes his living out of doors. I like the blue sky. I need people around me with the mentality and the wherewithal to spend money, if I am going to make money myself. I'm in a developing area, with people who have the money to spend and do spend it. Spain is where I expect to be for a long time to come. I hope I am here for the next 20 years because that will have proved that my instinct was right, and my decision to come to Spain was right—and it would compensate tremendously for my experience in Gloucestershire. That was a harsh lesson.

I have learned so much over the past 20 years, and at last I've cracked the code. I am looking forward eagerly to the next 20 years, sure I will not make the mistakes I made in the past but just as sure that I'll make other kinds of mistakes—maybe not so many because I hope I have learned to handle situations and people better. I have learned how to put issues into perspective better—you do as you grow older. I am no different from anyone else who reckons that by the time you are in your 40s you should have a fair measure of mature good sense!

Index